98

# 125 Best
# ICE CREAM
## Recipes

# 125 Best
# ICE CREAM
## Recipes

Marilyn Linton
and Tanya Linton

Robert
ROSE

For complete cataloguing information, see page 182.

Design & Production: PageWave Graphics Inc.
Editor: Carol Sherman
Copy Editor: Christina Anson Mine
Recipe Tester: Jennifer MacKenzie
Photography: Mark T. Shapiro
Food Stylist: Kate Bush
Props Stylist: Charlene Erricson
Color Scans: Colour Technologies

The publisher and authors wish to express their appreciation to the following supplier of props used in the food photography:
DISHES, LINENS AND ACCESSORIES
Homefront
371 Eglinton Ave. W.
Toronto, Ontario M5N 1A3
Tel: (416) 488-3189
www.homefrontshop.com

Cover image: Mango Ginger Ice (page 136)

We acknowledge the financial support of the Government of Canada through the Book Publishing Industry Development Program (BPIDP) for our publishing activities.

Published by: Robert Rose Inc.
120 Eglinton Ave. E., Suite 1000, Toronto, Ontario, Canada M4P 1E2
Tel: (416) 322-6552   Fax: (416) 322-6936

Printed in Canada
1 2 3 4 5 6 7 8 9 10   GP   09 08 07 06 05 04 03

# CONTENTS

# ✨ Acknowledgments

Writing a cookbook is a labor of love. Ideas need to be brainstormed. Ingredients need to be researched, and, most importantly, recipes need to be tested and tasted. We discovered that with ice cream as a topic, it wasn't very hard to find eager tasters to lick, slurp and sample various scoops. We couldn't have gotten through any of the stages of this book without the help of so many people.

For starters, this book would never have come to a freezer section near you if it weren't for the support of Bob Dees and the Robert Rose creative team. Thank you to our editor, Carol Sherman, who not only had enough patience to work with two Linton ladies, but whose diligent editing and coordinating of the manuscript helped us to get and keep our heads above water while meeting our deadlines. Thanks also to Jennifer MacKenzie, whose thoroughness and knowledge of testing enabled us to fine-tune our recipes, and to copy editor Tina Anson Mine. Of course, a cookbook just isn't the same without photos, and for those we are thankful to photographer Mark Shapiro, props stylist Charlene Erricson and food stylist Kate Bush, whose talent for preparing ice cream for use under hot lights cannot be underestimated. Thanks to designers Andrew Smith and Daniella Zanchetta at PageWave Graphics for making such a beautiful book.

When it came to researching the science of ice cream, we were grateful to Professor Douglas Goff in the Department of Food Science at the University of Guelph for his assistance, particularly in the area of freezing temperatures. We would also like to thank Cuisinart for giving us an ice cream maker so that we could whip up many of the desserts in this book.

We were also very fortunate to have Jim Borwick, our foodie family member, whose creative input, recipe testing and ice cream tasting enabled us to maintain our girlish figures. And last, but certainly not least, a big thank you goes out to our family, Doug Linton, Sam Linton, Charley Borwick and Sasha Borwick, who never tired of sampling and resampling the flavors found in this book.

# ✣ Introduction

LIKE EVERYONE ELSE IN THE WORLD, WE LOVE ICE CREAM. NOT ONLY is it the ultimate comfort food, one that's associated with fond memories of summer vacations and birthday parties, but it's also the ultimate treat, a little luxury that's affordable and easily available virtually anywhere in the world today. Thanks to the various ice cream makers that are now on the market, it's also the ideal food to make at home.

While each commercial manufacturer boasts dozens of flavors, we discovered to our delight that our made-at-home list was virtually limitless. The smaller batches produced in home ice cream makers get your creative juices flowing by inviting frequent experimentation. In trying everything from Apple Brown Betty Ice Cream (see recipe, page 24) to Beet Apple Slush (see recipe, page 121), we found — as we're sure you will — that inventing new flavor combinations is half the fun.

And because home ice cream makers incorporate less air into the mixture during the churning process than traditional big-batch commercial machines do, you're sure to get an ice cream that's creamier and fresher than store-bought. Ice cream was always meant to be eaten fresh, and there are even some ice cream aficionados who believe that storing it in the freezer compromises the flavor. We found that keeping it in the freezer for several days or even a week or two doesn't detract from the flavor too much, but nothing beats the taste of ice cream straight out of the machine or just a few hours old.

We think one of the reasons why ice cream makers are increasingly popular is that more and more of us are concerned about the components of our food. Homemade ice cream and its cousins — sherbets and ices — are about as wholesome as you can get. Not only do you start with the freshest eggs, milk, fruit and/or flavorings, but also, because you select them, you can make sure the ingredients are exactly what you want.

You can make it organic if that's important, low-fat if weight or cholesterol is an issue, or nut-free if allergies are a concern. Healthwise, ice cream, though it is about 14% fat, is a good source of both protein and calcium — the latter is essential for building and maintaining healthy bones in all of us, whatever our age. As well, most North American supermarkets now carry a good range of low-fat dairy (and non-dairy) products that decrease fat content without sacrificing taste. (Frozen yogurt, introduced in the 1970s and perceived by some as healthier than regular ice cream, is also a make-at-home option, particularly since the flavors available at the supermarket are still limited.) In each of our recipes, you are building your ice cream from the ground up, not relying on a commercial mix (even many ice cream shops that claim to make their own start with a mix).

We also found that ice cream is no longer confined to traditional flavors or enjoyed only in a sugar cone after dinner. In our ice cream travels, we learned that the sky's the limit as far as flavors go (the Roasted Garlic Ice Cream on page 94 is surprisingly good) and that ice cream isn't just a dessert (our healthy Tomato Basil Ice on page 147 makes that clear, as does one of our favorite breakfasts, waffles with Banana Ice Cream, on page 28.) Our serving suggestions will show you how to enhance your ice cream to fit into a party theme or mood.

That ice cream is such a simple food belies the fact that, sciencewise, it's a complex structure of ice crystals and fat globules. When conditions are right, they combine to make a frozen mixture with a good "mouth feel" to it — that is, a smooth, consistent texture rather than a coarse, grainy one. In our recipes, we provide the proper ratios of ingredients needed to achieve this, while leaving a little room for your own improvisation.

In writing this book, we discovered that homemade ice cream, when served to guests, can be more impressive than the fanciest cakes and tarts. Its appeal is universal, and it delights all ages and at all life stages. Kids are fascinated by the process of making homemade ice cream, and unlike other forms of cooking, in which sharp knives and hot stoves are a constant worry, managing an ice cream recipe is a relatively simple, anxiety-free task that kids and adults can share. After all, the ingredients are few, the cooking steps are straightforward and the end result is quickly achieved. We hope you and your family and friends will enjoy these recipes and that they'll give you the foundation and confidence to go on and create more of your own delicious flavors. Enjoy.

— Marilyn and Tanya Linton

# THE HISTORY OF ICE CREAM

If one of the measures of a food's success is its ability to go the distance, then ice cream has certainly passed the test of time. Just how far back it goes, no one really knows because much of the early history of ice cream remains unproven folklore. Though there are references that its beginnings may have reached as far back as ancient China, Persia and India, it's likely that ice cream evolved over centuries rather than having been invented on any particular day in any particular year. For instance, the Roman emperor Nero Claudius Caesar, who is said to have had an occasional craving for honey-flavored fruit-studded snow, sent his slaves into the mountains for the main ingredient.

In the 7th century, there are records of a Persian favorite: fruit-flavored crushed ice, known as *sharbat*, which was obviously a precursor to today's sherbet and not unlike the snow cones or flavored slushy refreshers typical to most modern fairgrounds. It's even likely that this sharbat was similar to a recipe the famed explorer Marco Polo is supposed to have brought back to Italy from China — if indeed he really did, for this may well be part of ice cream folklore. In ancient Greece and Turkey, concoctions similar to sharbat were also apparently enjoyed.

It is the Italians, however, who are credited with introducing ice cream to the rest of Europe. According to popular accounts, Catherine de' Medici, a Florentine who married Henry II of France in the mid-1500s, had her Italian chef make a variety of iced desserts — frozen thanks to icehouses, which were storage spaces (sometimes crude pits) for ice that was harvested. Part of the rich folklore surrounding ice cream also refers to an Italian chef who introduced ice cream to the British court.

In 1686, gelato (the Italian version of what in North America we call ice cream) found commercial success thanks to Sicilian Francesco Procopio dei Coltelli, who established Café Procope — a Parisian shrine to ice cream and coffee. In the United States, Dolley Madison, wife of President James Madison, is said to have served ice cream at her husband's inaugural ball. By the late 1800s, a recipe for homemade ice cream was published in an Italian cookbook: "Fill a bucket with crushed ice and salt. Set a second metal bucket with the ingredients in it and churn the ingredients vigorously for about an hour or until the mixture is creamy and smooth." In 1885, an Englishwoman, Agnes Marshall, wrote a whole book dedicated to ice cream.

# ICE CREAM MAKERS

Chill and stir: then, as now, these were the basic instructions for making ice cream. Today, nothing much has changed except that an electric machine can do the work instead of your arm, churning the mixture as it freezes and incorporating air into it. You can make ice cream in the freezer, using a metal cake pan, but the resulting texture is closer to that of frozen cream (tasty enough but not as appealing in its mouth feel). Scientists have also demonstrated that adding liquid nitrogen to flavored cream instantly produces ice cream, but this party trick is worth avoiding, since liquid nitrogen can burn exposed skin.

Price is certainly a factor to consider when purchasing an ice cream maker, but it's worth remembering that the easier the machine is to use and the faster it produces results, the more you will use it. Every machine has the basics: a bowl, a dasher (its churning paddles) and a freezing mechanism. There are basically four different kinds of units.

## Built-in compressor units

These top-of-the-line machines have their own built-in sealed fluorocarbon refrigerant systems. You put the chilled mixture into the machine's bowl, press the Chill and Churn buttons and, about 20 minutes later, are rewarded with supreme ice cream. These machines can churn out batches quickly, one after the other. Brand names to consider include Il Gelataio Magnum by Simac, the Robot Coupe Piccolo and Lussino (manufactured in Italy by Musso). These workhorses, most of which yield about 1 to $1\frac{1}{2}$ quarts (1 to 1.5 L) of ice cream, take up a little more counter space than other units but have removable canisters for easy washing. Though they make ice cream making truly effortless, their price tags (up to $800 each) are hefty.

## Manual and electric canister units

These ice cream makers have removable canisters lined with sealed liquid refrigerant, which you prefreeze. When you're ready to make ice cream, you insert the frozen canister into the machine, pour in the mixture and either flip the Churn switch or hand-crank the mixture. Some models freeze better than others, but we found that the smooth, dense texture of the ice cream produced by most of these machines didn't suffer if the last hour or two of freezing was done in a refrigerator freezer. Models are available in 1-pint (500 mL) or 1-quart (1 L) sizes. Prices are well under $100 (the hand-crank models are the least expensive). The only downside is that, because the canister liners take about eight to 10 hours to freeze, you are limited if you want to make more than one batch a day. Brand names to look for include Cuisinart, Donvier, Krups and Rival.

## Ice-and-rock-salt units

These old-fashioned ice cream makers (available in electric and hand-crank models) make airier ice cream because the churning process takes longer and incorporates more air into the mixture. Though not as readily available as canister units and not cheap (wooden ones cost over $150, but plastic versions are less), these units — especially the hand-cranked ones — provide an opportunity to closely observe the ice cream making process while illustrating the principle (somewhat like taking a boat instead of a plane overseas does) that not everything worth doing happens instantaneously. In these models, the combination of ice and salt is the freezing mechanism: salt interferes with ice crystallization and allows the temperature to drop below the freezing point of water. If you're using one of these units, a good ratio of salt to ice is 2 cups (500 mL) salt to 8 lbs (4 kg) ice cubes or crushed ice. Using more salt produces a coarser-textured ice cream, while using less salt and taking longer to churn makes for a silkier dessert. Machines vary in size. White Mountain is one brand name (for more information, contact them at 1-800-343-0065).

## Refrigerator freezers

Making ice cream in a refrigerator's freezer compartment is called "still freezing." But to avoid a rock-hard, unpleasant texture, you should manually incorporate air into the mixture by beating it several times during the freezing period. There are two popular methods. The first is to place the mixture in a metal loaf pan or square metal baking pan, cover it with plastic wrap and place it in the freezer until it is solid (about one to two hours); then, break the frozen mixture into pieces, spoon them into a food processor fitted with a metal blade and process until the mixture is soft but not melted. Repeat the freezing and processing a couple more times. The second method is to freeze the mixture until the edges are firm but the center is semisoft, then beat it with an electric mixer at medium-high speed until it is soft but not melted. Repeat the freezing and beating process a couple more times.

## OTHER EQUIPMENT

*Colander:* A large metal or plastic colander is suitable for washing soft fruits for these recipes.

*Food processor:* When it's necessary to purée fruit or combine ingredients very well before freezing, a food processor fitted with a metal blade works well.

*Grater:* For finely grated lime and lemon zest, we prefer to use a carpenter's rasp (now sold under the name "microplane grater" in kitchen stores) instead of a zester or traditional grater.

*Saucepan:* A medium-size heavy-bottomed saucepan, preferably nonstick, is all that's needed for most recipes that require you to cook the ice cream mixture.

*Sieve:* A medium-size nylon sieve or fine-mesh strainer is great for straining custards and removing seeds from berry mixtures.

*Spatula:* Many ice cream makers come with a plastic spatula-scoop that fits the curve of the machine's canister perfectly. A selection of spatulas will come in handy for scooping, scraping and spreading.

*Spoons:* Heatproof plastic spoons are preferable because they're unlikely to retain flavors, as wooden spoons can.

*Storage containers:* Storage containers in several sizes are available in supermarkets and hardware stores. We prefer solid plastic containers not unlike those used for take-out foods or yogurt.

*Whisks:* Wire whisks in different sizes are handy for stirring custards and combining fruit mixtures.

## PERFECT SCOOPS

You can get by using a sturdy tablespoon to scoop your ice cream at serving time, but a good ice cream scoop is worth the investment. Today, there are many styles to choose from. For sheer strength, we like the classic half-moon-shaped stainless-steel scoop. But visit any kitchen store and you will see much more variety — everything from simple metal spoon-shaped scoops with metal handles to easy-grip molded plastic scoops, some with quick-release levers built right in. The latest design has a nonstick, self-defrosting coating, which responds to the heat from your hand. For removing ice cream from the machine, we prefer a nonstick spade with a flat paddle-type head; this utensil is terrific for spreading and smoothing, as well. The trick to serving perfect scoops of ice cream that's a little hard is to first dip the scoop into hot water, then wipe it dry and quickly dip it into the ice cream. If you don't wipe it first, your scoop will be watery.

While serving the recipes in this book, we discovered that melon ballers are terrific tools, because we were often tasting many different preparations and wanted only a tiny scoop of each. Available from pea- to grape-size, melon ballers are also suitable for dinner-party desserts (guests may prefer a selection of miniature scoops instead of ice cream-cone-size ones).

## TYPES OF ICE CREAM

Is it gelato or ice cream, granita or ice? There's a lot of confusion surrounding these simple concoctions. In our research, we found the following definitions to be consistent.

### Ice cream
A creamy confection made from some combination of creams (as in heavy and light) or a combination of cream and whole milk, with or without eggs cooked into the mixture. A person's ice cream preference usually falls into either the egg-cream or all-cream (Philadelphia-style) category. As coauthors, we're split fifty-fifty.

### Ice milk
A lightened-up version of ice cream made from whole or partly skimmed milk (skim milk produces a too-thin taste), without eggs.

### Sherbet
A frozen dessert usually made from fruit purée and milk.

### Gelato
The word, derived from the Italian verb *gelare* (to freeze), is used for both ice cream and ice milk but is generally less than 7% butterfat; one popular gelato formula calls for a combination of 10% whipping cream

and 90% whole milk. Most gelatos contain 50% less air than most commercial ice creams, which gives them a smoother, denser texture.

## Granita
These Italian-style water-based dairy-free ices are generally made with sugar syrup and flavored with fruit juices, coffee, tea or herbs and have a snowlike texture (granita is from the Italian word for "grain"). Granitas are made using the still-freezing method, which requires that the mixture be stirred several times during freezing to create the proper ice crystals.

## Ice
A blend of puréed fruit or vegetables with water or sugar syrup, frozen by machine to a smooth texture. Figure on using 5 cups (1.25 L) of berries or fruit to produce about 2 cups (500 mL) of purée.

# FAT CONTENT

## Regular ice cream
To be called ice cream, a product must have a butterfat content of at least 10%.

## Low-fat
Low-fat usually means 3 grams of fat or less per serving.

## Light
This term often means that the product contains 50% less fat than the same brand's regular ice cream.

## Non-fat
For a product to be non-fat, it must contain less than 0.5 grams of fat per serving.

# A LOT OF AIR

Air is incorporated into ice cream during the freezing process; the amount of air incorporated is called "overrun" in commercial ice cream. Without it, ice cream would be nothing but a frozen brick. Commercial overrun percentages can range from 21% to close to 100%. Low overrun produces denser, creamier ice cream and is what you're likely to get with your home ice cream maker. High overrun results in a product that is very light and pillowy and melts quite quickly. In addition to air, commercially made ice cream contains emulsifiers, such as mono- and diglycerides, to prevent the fat from separating from the ice cream mass. Carob, carrageenan and guar gum are all popular stabilizers used to prevent the formation of ice crystals in low-fat mixtures and protect against heat shock caused by changes in temperature that take place in transit.

## INGREDIENTS

As with all cooking-from-scratch recipes, we use only the freshest and finest ingredients. Here are the most common.

*Simple syrup:* This is the basis for many of our ices, sherbets, gelatos and ice creams. This sugar syrup is a combination of one part sugar to one part water that's heated until the sugar dissolves, then cooled. You can make it in large batches and store it in the refrigerator for up to three months so it's ready when needed (see recipe, page 23).

*Corn syrup:* Used in some recipes as a sweetener, it helps create a light, smooth texture.

### Cream

*Whipping (35%) cream:* Sometimes called heavy cream, this full-fat cream is essential on its own or in combination with a lower-fat cream, such as half-and-half, or milk to make ice cream. Though ice cream can be made by adding whipped cream to the final churnings of the remaining ingredients, we prefer to add it in its liquid state.

*Table (18%) cream:* This cream, commonly used in coffee, is lower in fat than whipping cream and is used extensively in ice cream making.

*Half-and-half (10%) cream:* This mixture of milk and cream is a good substitute for table cream in recipes.

*Sour cream:* Its slightly tart flavor and smooth texture are nice paired with many fruits, especially blueberries, and make rich ice cream. Though sour cream is now available in reduced-fat and non-fat varieties, the best ice cream uses the full-fat version.

### Milk

*Whole milk:* We prefer whole homogenized milk (3.3% fat), though reduced-fat (2%) works well, especially when combined with whole milk or light cream. Avoid 1% or skim milk, as they deliver very little taste when frozen. Lactose-free milk can be substituted.

*Non-fat powdered milk:* Though not an ingredient used in most kitchens, powdered milk is economical and needs no refrigeration until it is reconstituted with water.

*Evaporated milk:* Available in cans, evaporated milk is more concentrated than whole milk; use it undiluted.

*Sweetened condensed milk:* Unlike evaporated milk, this is concentrated milk with a large amount of added sugar; when called for, use it undiluted.

*Yogurt:* Milk that has fermented and coagulated through the addition of beneficial bacteria, yogurt comes in plain, flavored, low-fat and fat-free varieties. The higher the fat, the more stable the product.

*Goat's milk:* Goat's milk makes an interesting ice cream with a distinctive taste that's not unlike that of goat cheese. Try it paired with honey or flavored with blueberries or dried cranberries.

*Soy beverage:* An alternative for anyone who dislikes or is allergic to dairy, soy beverages come sweetened or unsweetened, plain or flavored.

*Coconut milk:* Used today to add an Asian and Caribbean flavor to food, canned coconut milk is a liquid made from the flesh of the coconut.

*Cheeses:* Low-fat fromage frais is fresh white cheese made with whole or skim milk and cream. It has the consistency of cream cheese, with fewer calories and less cholesterol, and is terrific when added to fruit-based ice creams. The soft, creamy texture of ricotta and the richness of mascarpone also provide excellent flavor. Cheeses are best added to ice cream that is semifrozen, because their high fat content can make the ice cream too buttery if they're churned too long.

## Other Ingredients

*Eggs:* We use large eggs. Egg safety: Use only fresh eggs that have been stored in the refrigerator. If you find a cracked egg in the carton, throw it out. In the egg-based ice creams in this book, we suggest you cook the eggs together with the milk or cream to at least 160°F (70°C). Though the risk of salmonella in uncooked eggs is low, the illness is a serious one. Better to be safe than sorry.

*Gelatin:* We add gelatin to some recipes to help create a smooth texture.

*Chocolate:* Throughout this book, we suggest you buy good-quality chocolate for your ices and ice cream mixtures. Here are some things to consider.

- Buy chocolate from a retailer whose products turn over quickly and don't sit on the shelf. Make sure that the chocolate package looks new and not dusty.

- Old chocolate can look pale and powdery (this is called bloom) because of being stored in an overly warm place. You can still use it. The flavor and texture are only slightly changed.

- Bittersweet chocolate is made from chocolate liquor sweetened with sugar and is blended with additional cocoa butter. Look for chocolate with at least 35% chocolate liquor.

## QUANTITY

Each recipe in this book makes about 1 quart (1 L). However, because ice cream makers incorporate different amounts of air and so many other factors, including the freezing method and the temperature of the ingredients prior to freezing, affect the final yield, you may get a little more or a little less with each recipe. Generally speaking, 1 quart (1 L) is enough for six adults.

## HYGIENE AND FOOD SAFETY

Ice cream makers and any utensils used during the process of making ice cream or ices should be kept scrupulously clean by washing in hot soapy water and rinsing in hot water. All dairy ingredients should be cold. When making an egg custard as an ice cream base, we recommend that you cook the custard to 185°F (85°C) to kill bacteria. It's important to keep stirring the custard to ensure that the eggs don't curdle, but if they do, a good remedy is to strain the custard through a fine sieve when you have finished cooking it.

Every cooked custard must be cooled before it can be transferred to an ice cream maker. To minimize the potential for bacterial growth, put the pan containing the hot custard into a bowl of ice water and stir it occasionally until it's room temperature and cool enough to refrigerate.

To further minimize the risk of illness, we recommend using powdered egg whites instead of fresh ones when egg whites are called for.

## STORAGE

Store each batch in a freezerproof container (we found that most plastic take-out tubs work just fine) in the main part of your freezer, not on your freezer door. Commercially, ice cream is stored at three different temperatures: The deep freeze (−15 to −22°F/−26 to −30°C) is used when the product is first made. In its distribution phase and for supermarket storage, the temperature is −4°F (−20°C) or less. In the display case, from which your ice cream is usually served at an ice cream shop, the storage is a little warmer (about 4 to 7°F/−16 to −14°C) so the ice cream can be scooped easily. To make ice cream at home, you should be able to get the temperature to 18 to 21°F (−8 to −6°C) in the machine, then harden it in your home freezer, which is usually in the −4°F (−20°C) range.

When filling a plastic tub with ice cream, leave about $\frac{1}{4}$ inch (0.5 cm) headspace to allow for any increase in volume that occurs during the freezing process. Also, place a piece of plastic wrap on top of the ice cream before putting the lid of the tub on; this provides an excellent seal against any moisture and keeps the surface from drying out.

## HOW MUCH ALCOHOL?

Using too much alcohol in a recipe prevents ice cream or ices from freezing well. Use the following as your guide: for 4 cups (1 L) base mixture, use less than 1 cup (250 mL) wine of up to 12% alcohol, up to $\frac{1}{2}$ cup (125 mL) dessert wine or liqueur of up to 25% alcohol, or up to $\frac{1}{4}$ cup (50 mL) distilled alcohol of up to 48% alcohol.

## PERFECT ICE CREAM

We evaluate ice cream, like wine, according to certain criteria, including appearance, texture, flavor and meltability.

Appearance is the most obvious, and it's undoubtedly an important attribute when you consider the role your eyes play in choosing one ice cream over another among tubs on display in an ice cream shop. A good ice cream is devoid of ice crystals and has no evidence of shrinkage from the sides of its container. Any nuts, raisins or candies mixed in should be evenly distributed. The color is less important; for instance, some people like pistachio ice cream a pale natural green, while others like the neon color that results from the addition of green food coloring.

The texture of an ice cream or an ice should be smooth. Visible ice crystals indicate that the ice cream is too old, has been poorly mixed or contains the wrong ratio of ingredients.

We think the flavor should be true to itself. Strawberry should taste like the real berry, chocolate should be made from the finest chocolate. The balance is important: some ice creams are overpowering in their flavor, and the pleasure of wanting more than a spoonful or two is therefore denied. On the other hand, some flavors are so limp and weak that virtually all you can taste is the frozen milk or cream. We find that the acceptability of sweetness is subjective, but ice cream or ices that are overly sweet can obliterate any flavor, which is truly unfortunate.

Finally, meltability is important. One of our failures (the recipe was obviously scrapped) was an ice cream that remained rock-solid despite standing for 10 minutes at room temperature. Ice cream should melt to a creamy puddle, ice to a pool of flavored water.

# WHY YOUR ICE CREAM WON'T FREEZE AND OTHER PROBLEMS

### When your ice cream finishes in a semifrozen, not frozen, state.

Many home ice cream makers produce softer ice cream than is found in commercial products — and many people prefer their ice cream this way. To harden, or "ripen," an ice cream before serving, transfer it from the machine to a freezerproof container, then place it in the freezer until it achieves the consistency you prefer.

### When your ice cream has large ice crystals.

If the temperature of the prepared ingredients was below 40°F (5°C) when the freezing began, the mixture may have frozen too fast and not allowed the machine to incorporate enough air.

### When your ice cream has hardened in the freezer to a rock-solid mass.

Because homemade ice creams contain no commercial stabilizers, they will freeze harder even though they may have been soft straight out of the machine. Check the firmness of your ice cream an hour before serving time. If it's rock-solid, temper it by placing it in the refrigerator for 10 to 15 minutes. To soften ice cream even faster, spoon it into the bowl of a food processor fitted with a metal blade and whirl it until it is smooth but not melted. Or beat it with an electric mixer until soft.

## TOP LICKS

*In 2001, the Top 5 flavors of ice cream in the United States were vanilla, chocolate, Neapolitan, butter pecan and chocolate chip.*

# ICE CREAMS

# Simple Syrup

## MAKES 3 CUPS (750 mL)

**Tip:** The reduced-sugar version will produce a firmer texture when added to ices and sorbets and then frozen. Recipes made with this version are best served right away, softened slightly before scooping or scraped into a shaved granita-style dessert.

*This recipe is the basis of many of the frozen desserts in this book. It's easy to make, and you can cover and keep it in the refrigerator for up to three months. We also use it to sweeten iced tea, limeade and lemonade. For a less sweet version, decrease the sugar to 1 cup (250 mL), see Tip, left. Double the recipe to make a larger quantity if you plan to make lots of ice cream or ices in the next couple of months.*

| 2 cups | granulated sugar | 500 mL |
| 2 cups | water | 500 mL |

1. In a medium saucepan over medium-low heat, bring sugar and water to a simmer. Cook, stirring, for 1 minute or until sugar is completely dissolved. Simmer, without stirring, for 2 minutes more.

2. Transfer to an airtight container and refrigerate until cold.

# Apple Brown Betty Ice Cream

**SERVES 6 TO 8**

*Apple butter isn't just for toast, as we discovered in this ice cream that offers a definite taste of autumn in Canada. We also like it served on crêpes for brunch. Rich and spicy gingersnaps give it texture and color.*

**Tip:** To cook custard: Cook over low heat, stirring constantly, for about 15 minutes. When custard thickens and coats the back of a wooden spoon without dripping, it's ready. A good way to test thickness is to drag your finger along the back of the coated spoon to see if a line appears.

**Serving suggestions:** Serve in hollowed-out apples and dust with cinnamon sugar.

For a Halloween treat, drizzle top with melted chocolate in a spiderweb pattern.

| | | |
|---|---|---:|
| 1 cup | granulated sugar | 250 mL |
| 2 | eggs | 2 |
| 1 | egg yolk | 1 |
| 2 tsp | all-purpose flour | 10 mL |
| 1 cup | table (18%) cream | 250 mL |
| 1 1/2 cups | apple butter | 375 mL |
| 1/2 tsp | ground cinnamon | 2 mL |
| 1 tsp | vanilla | 5 mL |
| 1 cup | whipping (35%) cream | 250 mL |
| 1 cup | crumbled gingersnaps | 250 mL |

1. In a bowl, whisk together sugar, eggs and egg yolk until thickened and pale yellow. Whisk in flour. Set aside.

2. In a medium saucepan over medium-low heat, bring table cream to a simmer. Gradually whisk into egg mixture. Return entire mixture to the saucepan. Cook over low heat, stirring constantly, until the mixture is thick enough to coat the back of a wooden spoon (see Tip, left). Be careful not to let it boil or the eggs will scramble.

3. Remove from heat and whisk in apple butter and cinnamon. Strain into a clean large bowl. Add vanilla. Cover and refrigerate until completely cold or overnight.

4. Stir in whipping cream. Transfer to an ice cream maker and freeze according to manufacturer's instructions. In the last 5 minutes of freezing, add crumbled gingersnaps and let machine stir them in.

5. Ice cream will be soft. For firmer ice cream, place in the freezer for at least 2 hours.

**VARIATION:** *Instead of the gingersnaps, 1 cup (250 mL) cinnamon granola would also be yummy and would add a nice texture to the ice cream.*

# Apricot Ice Cream

**SERVES 6**

**Tip:** For an extra-fruity version, you can finely chop your favorite fruit leather and add it in the last 5 minutes of freezing.

**Serving suggestion:** Although Apricot Ice Cream is satisfying on its own, when scooped into a chocolate cup it's transformed into a dinner-party dazzler. Chocolate cups are available in supermarkets. Their small cup-like shapes make for elegant desserts.

*We recommend using canned apricots, but you can also use fresh ones that have been peeled and pitted. The addition of dried apricots, however, is important, because it amplifies the flavor.*

| | | |
|---|---|---|
| $^1/_2$ cup | chopped dried apricots | 125 mL |
| $^1/_2$ cup | Simple Syrup (see recipe, page 23) | 125 mL |
| 2 | cans (each 14 oz/398 mL) apricots in syrup | 2 |
| 1 tbsp | freshly squeezed lemon juice | 15 mL |
| 1 cup | whipping (35%) cream | 250 mL |

1. In a small bowl, combine dried apricots and syrup. Let soak for 15 minutes.

2. In a food processor or blender, purée dried apricot mixture, canned apricots with syrup and lemon juice until smooth.

3. Transfer to a clean large bowl. Stir in cream.

4. Transfer to an ice cream maker and freeze according to manufacturer's instructions.

> **VARIATION:** ***Prune Ice Cream:*** *Substitute 1 cup (250 mL) pitted dried prunes soaked in the Simple Syrup for both the dried apricots and canned apricots.*

# Avocado
# Ice Cream

**SERVES 8 TO 10**

*This popular South American dessert promises not only a beautiful color but also a velvety texture. Make sure you use the ripest avocados you can find. Treat this as an adventure in flavor and complement it with a scoop of traditional vanilla or chocolate ice cream.*

**Serving suggestion:** Melon ballers, available in various sizes, are very handy for serving small scoops of ice cream (which may be appealing after a large dinner). Pile small scoops of a single flavor in a bowl or present a variety of different flavors on an ice cream tasting plate.

| | | |
|---|---|---|
| 4 | ripe avocados, peeled, pitted and chopped (about 2 cups/500 mL) | 4 |
| 1 cup | whipping (35%) cream | 250 mL |
| 1/2 cup | granulated sugar | 125 mL |
| 1/4 cup | freshly squeezed lime juice | 50 mL |

1. In a food processor or blender, purée avocados, cream, sugar and lime juice until smooth.

2. Transfer to an ice cream maker and freeze according to manufacturer's instructions.

# Banana Ice Cream

*Use the ripest bananas you can find for this recipe. It's luscious on its own but even more decadent with $1/2$ cup (125 mL) toasted chopped pecans or walnuts added in the last five minutes of freezing.*

**SERVES 6**

**Tip:** If you have a real sweet tooth, you can increase the sugar to $2/3$ cup (150 mL).

**Serving suggestions:** For bananaholics, serve a scoop of Banana Ice Cream on a bed of sliced bananas. Top with whipped cream, chocolate sauce and a maraschino cherry. Or (for adults only) splash on a bit of banana liqueur.

| 2 | eggs | 2 |
|---|---|---|
| $1/2$ cup | granulated sugar | 125 mL |
| I tbsp | all-purpose flour | 15 mL |
| $1^{1}/2$ cups | table (18%) cream | 375 mL |
| 3 | large ripe bananas | 3 |
| $1/4$ cup | milk | 50 mL |
| I tsp | freshly squeezed lemon juice | 5 mL |
| I tsp | vanilla | 5 mL |

1. In a bowl, whisk eggs with sugar until thickened and pale yellow. Whisk in flour. Set aside.

2. In a medium saucepan over medium-low heat, bring cream to a simmer. Gradually whisk into the egg mixture.

3. Return entire mixture to the saucepan. Cook over low heat, stirring constantly, until the mixture is thick enough to coat the back of a wooden spoon. Be careful not to let it boil. Strain into a clean large bowl. Let cool to room temperature.

4. In a food processor or blender, purée bananas with milk until smooth. Pour into cream mixture, scraping down the side of the bowl. Stir in lemon juice and vanilla. Cover and refrigerate until completely cold or overnight.

5. Stir cream mixture. Transfer to an ice cream maker and freeze according to manufacturer's instructions.

---

**VARIATION:** *Banana Mocha Ice Cream:* Add $1/2$ cup (125 mL) shaved chocolate in the last 5 minutes of freezing. For a touch of coffee, add $1/4$ cup (50 mL) chocolate-covered espresso beans in the last 5 minutes of freezing.

# Banana Toffee Ice Cream

## SERVES 6 TO 8

*This ice cream features an unbeatable combination that's favored by our Scottish friends, who call it "banoffee ice cream." You can use your favorite brand of chewy or hard toffee for this recipe. Sweetened condensed milk gives it a cheesecake-like flavor.*

| | | |
|---|---|---|
| 3 | large ripe bananas | 3 |
| | Juice of 1 lemon | |
| 1 | can (10 oz/300 mL) sweetened condensed milk | 1 |
| 1⅓ cups | whipping (35%) cream | 325 mL |
| 2 | packages (each 4 oz/112 g) toffee, chopped into ¼-inch (0.5 cm) squares | 2 |

**Tips:** This ice cream will be soft. For firmer ice cream, place in the freezer for at least 2 hours.

If you plan to serve this recipe to small children, either leave out the toffee (because it's too sharp and can cause choking) or substitute the same amount of butterscotch chips for it.

1. In a food processor or blender, purée bananas until smooth. Add lemon juice and sweetened condensed milk. Process until combined.

2. Transfer to a clean large bowl. Stir in cream. Cover and refrigerate until completely cold or overnight.

3. Stir cream mixture. Transfer to an ice cream maker and freeze according to manufacturer's instructions. Add toffee in the last 5 minutes of freezing and let machine stir it in.

> **VARIATION:** *Banana Chocolate Toffee Ice Cream: For extra texture, add ¼ cup (50 mL) chocolate chips.*

# Brown Bread Ice Cream

**SERVES 6**

*Though unusual, this ice cream is one of the best we've ever had. Because the bread crumbs are caramelized, the result is more like pralines than bread pudding.*

**Tips:** We have used 2% milk here and in several other recipes. Not only does it reduce the fat content, but it tastes just as good as whole milk. If you prefer a full-fat version, use whole milk instead.

The success of this ice cream depends on the whole wheat bread. Don't substitute white bread for it.

**Serving suggestion:** Like your favorite bread pudding, this ice cream is amazing drizzled with buttery Sticky Sauce (see recipe, page 180).

| | | |
|---|---|---|
| 4 | egg yolks | 4 |
| 1/3 cup | granulated sugar | 75 mL |
| 1 1/2 cups | 2% milk (see Tips, left) | 375 mL |
| 1 cup | whipping (35%) cream | 250 mL |
| 1 tsp | lemon zest | 5 mL |
| 1 tsp | vanilla | 5 mL |
| 3 tbsp | unsalted butter | 45 mL |
| 1 1/2 cups | fresh whole wheat bread crumbs | 375 mL |
| 1/2 cup | packed brown sugar | 125 mL |

1. In a bowl, whisk egg yolks with sugar until thickened and pale yellow. Set aside.

2. In a medium saucepan over medium-low heat, bring milk to a simmer. Gradually whisk into the egg mixture.

3. Return entire mixture to the saucepan. Cook over low heat, stirring constantly, until the mixture is thick enough to coat the back of a wooden spoon. Be careful not to let it boil. Strain into a clean large bowl. Let cool to room temperature.

4. Stir in cream, lemon zest and vanilla. Cover and refrigerate until completely cold or overnight.

5. Meanwhile, in another medium saucepan over medium heat, melt butter. Add bread crumbs and brown sugar. Cook, stirring, for 4 to 5 minutes or until golden brown and bread crumbs are evenly coated. Drain on paper towel-lined plate.

6. Stir cream mixture. Transfer to an ice cream maker and freeze according to manufacturer's instructions. Add bread-crumb mixture in the last 5 minutes of freezing and let machine stir it in.

# Brown Sugar Ice Cream

*This ice cream is even sweeter than most. The taste is similar to that of light molasses — and equally good.*

**SERVES 4 TO 6**

**Tips:** This ice cream will be soft. For firmer ice cream, place in the freezer for at least 2 hours.

Egg safety: Use only fresh eggs that have been stored in the refrigerator. If you find a cracked egg in the carton, throw it out. In the egg-based ice creams in this book, we suggest that you cook the eggs together with the milk or cream to at least 160°F (70°C). Though the risk of salmonella in uncooked eggs is low, the illness is a serious one. Better to be safe than sorry.

| 4 | egg yolks | 4 |
| --- | --- | --- |
| ¾ cup | packed brown sugar | 175 mL |
| 1½ cups | table (18%) cream | 375 mL |
| ½ cup | 2% milk (see Tips, page 30) | 125 mL |
| 1 cup | whipping (35%) cream | 250 mL |
| 2 tsp | vanilla | 10 mL |
| Pinch | salt | Pinch |

1. In a bowl, whisk egg yolks with sugar until thickened and pale yellow. Set aside.

2. In a medium saucepan over medium-low heat, bring table cream and milk to a simmer. Gradually whisk into the egg mixture.

3. Return entire mixture to the saucepan. Cook over low heat, stirring constantly, until the mixture is thick enough to coat the back of a wooden spoon. Be careful not to let it boil. Strain into a clean large bowl. Let cool to room temperature.

4. Stir in whipping cream, vanilla and salt. Cover and refrigerate until completely cold or overnight.

5. Stir cream mixture. Transfer to an ice cream maker and freeze according to manufacturer's instructions.

# Butter Pecan Ice Cream

**SERVES 6**

**Tip:** This ice cream will be soft. For firmer ice cream, place in the freezer for at least 2 hours.

**Serving suggestions:** For an elegant finish to a barbecue, sandwich a scoop of Butter Pecan Ice Cream between two flat cookies (preferably chocolate chip) and freeze until firm. Or spoon a simple caramel sauce over a scoop. Although most cookies are flat, it is better to make ice cream sandwiches with flat, wide cookies instead of small, domed ones.

*You say pe-can, we say pe-cahn. However you pronounce it, this recipe is a classic. For extra crunchiness, toast the pecans before adding to the mixture.*

| | | |
|---|---|---|
| 2 | eggs | 2 |
| $1/4$ cup | unsalted butter | 50 mL |
| I cup | packed brown sugar | 250 mL |
| I cup | table (18%) cream | 250 mL |
| $1/2$ cup | milk | 125 mL |
| I cup | whipping (35%) cream | 250 mL |
| I tsp | vanilla | 5 mL |
| $1/4$ tsp | almond extract | I mL |
| $1\,1/2$ cups | pecan halves | 375 mL |

1. In a bowl, whisk eggs until pale yellow. Set aside.

2. In a medium saucepan over medium heat, melt butter. Cook, stirring, until it begins to brown and smell slightly nutty. Add brown sugar. Stir until melted. Reduce heat to low. Add table cream and milk and bring to a simmer. Gradually whisk into the eggs.

3. Return entire mixture to the saucepan. Cook over low heat, stirring constantly, until the mixture is thick enough to coat the back of a wooden spoon. Be careful not to let it boil. Strain into a clean large bowl. Let cool to room temperature.

4. Stir in whipping cream, vanilla and almond extract. Cover and refrigerate until completely cold or overnight.

5. Stir cream mixture. Transfer to an ice cream maker and freeze according to manufacturer's instructions.

6. Add pecans in the last 5 minutes of freezing and let machine stir them in.

Classic Chocolate Ice Cream (page 42)

# Café au Lait Ice Cream

**SERVES 8 TO 10**

*Nothing beats warm milk infused with coffee — nothing except the ice cream version of the popular drink. This buzz-a-licious dessert is so addictive that we've caught people eating it right out of the container in the middle of the night.*

**Serving suggestion:** For a trendy refresher, make this coffee frosty by placing two scoops of Café au Lait Ice Cream in a beer mug. Top with freshly brewed strong coffee. Garnish with a cinnamon stick.

| | | |
|---|---|---|
| 8 | egg yolks | 8 |
| 1 ½ cups | packed brown sugar | 375 mL |
| 4 cups | milk | I L |
| 2 cups | whipping (35%) cream | 500 mL |
| 1 cup | freshly brewed strong coffee | 250 mL |

1. In a bowl, whisk egg yolks with sugar until thickened and pale yellow. Set aside.

2. In a medium saucepan over medium-low heat, bring milk and whipping cream to a simmer. Gradually whisk into the egg mixture.

3. Return entire mixture to the saucepan. Cook over low heat, stirring constantly, until the mixture is thick enough to coat the back of a wooden spoon. Be careful not to let it boil. Strain into a clean large bowl. Let cool to room temperature.

4. Stir in coffee. Cover and refrigerate until completely cold or overnight.

5. Stir cream mixture. Transfer to an ice cream maker and freeze according to manufacturer's instructions.

> **VARIATION:** *Chocolate Coffee Ice Cream: Stir in 6 oz (175 g) bittersweet chocolate, melted, just before the mixture goes into the ice cream maker.*

*Dulce de Leche Ice Cream (page 56)*

# Café Mocha Ice Cream

**SERVES 6 TO 8**

*We make this with espresso beans, but any dark roast will make just as delicious a dessert. For extra-strong flavor, place the beans in a plastic bag, seal the bag and lightly crush them with a rolling pin before adding them to the heated cream to steep.*

**Tip:** Melting chocolate is very easy but requires close attention because it can burn quickly. Our method is to melt it in the top half of a double boiler over simmering water. If you don't have a double boiler, use a saucepan and a stainless-steel bowl. Pour in enough water to come 1 inch (2.5 cm) up side of saucepan. Bring to a simmer over medium heat. Place chocolate in bowl. Place over pan and stir until melted.

| | | |
|---|---|---|
| 2 cups | whipping (35%) cream | 500 mL |
| 1 cup | espresso or dark-roasted coffee beans | 250 mL |
| 1 cup | milk | 250 mL |
| 6 | egg yolks | 6 |
| 1/2 cup | granulated sugar | 125 mL |
| 4 oz | bittersweet chocolate, melted (see Tip, left) | 125 g |
| 1 tbsp | coffee-flavored liqueur (optional) | 15 mL |

1. In a medium saucepan over medium-low heat, bring cream, espresso beans and milk just to a boil. Remove from heat and let stand for 1 hour. Strain into a bowl and set aside.

2. In a separate bowl, whisk egg yolks with sugar until thickened and pale yellow. Set aside.

3. Return cream mixture to the saucepan. Bring to a simmer over medium-low heat. Gradually whisk into the egg mixture.

4. Return entire mixture to the saucepan. Cook over low heat, stirring constantly, until the mixture is thick enough to coat the back of a wooden spoon. Be careful not to let it boil. Strain into a clean large bowl. Let cool to room temperature.

5. Stir in melted chocolate. Cover and refrigerate until completely cold or overnight.

6. Stir cream mixture. Transfer to an ice cream maker and freeze according to manufacturer's instructions. Add coffee-flavored liqueur, if using, in the last 5 minutes of freezing and let machine stir it in.

**VARIATION:** *Chocolate Espresso Bean Ice Cream: Add ½ cup (125 mL) chocolate-covered espresso beans in the last 5 minutes of freezing and let machine stir them in.*

# Caramel Ice Cream

**SERVES 4 TO 6**

**Tip:** To make vanilla sugar, place vanilla pod in an airtight container with granulated sugar. Store for 1 week to let flavor infuse. Use to flavor whipped cream, custards or dessert sauces.

**Serving suggestion:** Line a 9-by 5-inch (1.5 L) loaf pan with plastic wrap. Spread 4 cups (1 L) softened Caramel Ice Cream in pan. Smooth top with a spatula. Freeze for 1 hour or until firm. Cover ice cream with 4 cups (1 L) softened chocolate ice cream. Smooth top. Freeze for 1 hour or until firm. To serve, unwrap and turn out of pan onto a cutting board. Using a knife dipped in hot water, cut into slices.

*This good old-fashioned custard cream is very rich, but it's also very rewarding with its wonderful taste. We love this ice cream with bananas sautéed with brown sugar, butter and a dash of rum.*

| | | |
|---|---|---|
| 1 | vanilla bean | 1 |
| 6 | egg yolks | 6 |
| 1 cup | granulated sugar | 250 mL |
| ¼ cup | water | 50 mL |
| 1 cup | whipping (35%) cream | 250 mL |
| 1 cup | milk | 250 mL |

1. Slit vanilla bean lengthwise. Scrape seeds into a bowl. Discard pod or make vanilla sugar for later use (see Tip, left). Whisk in egg yolks until pale yellow. Set aside.

2. In a medium saucepan over medium-low heat, stir sugar with water until sugar is dissolved. Cook, stirring constantly, until deep amber color.

3. Remove from heat. (Be careful to avert your face and hold the saucepan away from you because cold cream meeting hot caramel means dangerous spatters.) Add cream and milk, stirring until foaming subsides. Return to heat. Cook, stirring constantly, for 5 minutes or until a velvety caramel sauce forms. Gradually whisk into the egg mixture.

4. Transfer entire mixture to a clean saucepan. Cook over low heat, stirring constantly, until the mixture is thick enough to coat the back of a wooden spoon. Be careful not to let it boil. Strain into a clean large bowl. Let cool to room temperature. Cover and refrigerate until completely cold or overnight.

5. Stir cream mixture. Transfer to an ice cream maker and freeze according to manufacturer's instructions.

# Cashew Ice Cream

**SERVES 6**

**Tip:** To toast nuts, spread them in a thin layer in a metal cake pan or on a rimmed baking sheet. Toast in 350°F (180°C) oven, watching carefully to prevent burning or overbrowning, for 3 to 5 minutes or until golden and fragrant. Let cool to room temperature.

**Serving suggestion:** Give this ice cream a fiery bite with the following topping. Toss together ¼ cup (50 mL) unsalted cashews, 2 tbsp (25 mL) corn syrup and ¼ tsp (1 mL) cayenne pepper. Spread on a rimmed baking sheet. Bake in 350°F (180°C) oven for 5 minutes or until golden. Let cool. Chop and sprinkle over ice cream.

*This rich, buttery ice cream is luxuriously sweet and nutty. For a little variety, add 2 tbsp (25 mL) each sunflower seeds, raisins and chopped dates to the machine in the last 5 minutes of freezing.*

| | | |
|---|---|---|
| 2 | eggs | 2 |
| 1½ cups | 2% milk (see Tips, page 30) | 375 mL |
| 1 cup | whipping (35%) cream | 250 mL |
| ¾ cup | Simple Syrup (see recipe, page 23) | 175 mL |
| 1 tsp | orange zest | 5 mL |
| ¼ tsp | vanilla | 1 mL |
| 1 cup | finely chopped unsalted cashews, toasted (see Tip, left) | 250 mL |

1. In a large bowl, whisk eggs until pale yellow. Set aside.

2. In a medium saucepan over medium-low heat, bring milk and cream to a simmer. Gradually whisk into the eggs.

3. Return entire mixture to the saucepan. Cook over low heat, stirring constantly, until the mixture is thick enough to coat the back of a wooden spoon. Be careful not to let it boil. Strain into a clean large bowl. Let cool to room temperature.

4. Stir in syrup, orange zest and vanilla. Cover and refrigerate until completely cold or overnight.

5. Stir cream mixture. Transfer to an ice cream maker and freeze according to manufacturer's instructions. Add cashews in the last 5 minutes of freezing.

**VARIATION:** *Cashew Raisin Ice Cream: Decrease cashews to ½ cup (125 mL) and add ½ cup (125 mL) golden raisins to the chilled cream mixture.*

# Cherries and Cream Ice Cream

## SERVES 4

**Tip:** If you're using fresh cherries, make sure they're plump and ripe. The best way to remove their pits is to invest in a cherry pitter. These inexpensive timesaving gadgets can be found at many hardware stores and most kitchen stores.

*If you prefer non-custardy ice cream, this is a wonderful and simple recipe that also works well with summer's fresh dark, sweet, juicy fruit.*

| | | |
|---|---|---|
| 1 cup | whipping (35%) cream | 250 mL |
| 1/2 cup | milk | 125 mL |
| 1/2 cup | granulated sugar | 125 mL |
| 1 cup | pitted fresh sweet cherries or 1 can (14 oz/398 mL) pitted sweet cherries, drained (see Tip, left) | 250 mL |

1. In a medium saucepan over medium-low heat, bring cream and milk to a simmer. Add sugar and cook, stirring, until sugar is dissolved. Be careful not to let it boil. Strain into a clean large bowl. Let cool to room temperature.

2. In a food processor or blender, purée cherries until smooth. Stir into cream mixture. Cover and refrigerate until completely cold or overnight.

3. Stir cream mixture. Transfer to an ice cream maker and freeze according to manufacturer's instructions.

# Cherry Custard Ice Cream

*Enjoy the summery taste of cherries year-round with this luscious recipe. You could use fresh cherries, but why not save them for eating and use frozen or canned cherries here instead.*

**SERVES 6**

| | | |
|---|---|---|
| 2 | egg yolks | 2 |
| ¾ cup | granulated sugar | 175 mL |
| I cup | milk | 250 mL |
| I | can (I4 oz/398 mL) pitted sweet cherries in syrup | I |
| I ½ cups | whipping (35%) cream | 375 mL |

1. In a bowl, whisk egg yolks with sugar until thickened and pale yellow. Set aside.

2. In a medium saucepan over medium-low heat, bring milk to a simmer. Gradually whisk into the egg mixture.

3. Return entire mixture to the saucepan. Cook over low heat, stirring constantly, until the mixture is thick enough to coat the back of a wooden spoon. Be careful not to let it boil. Strain into a clean large bowl. Let cool to room temperature.

4. In a food processor or blender, purée cherries with syrup until almost smooth. Stir cherry mixture along with cream into milk mixture. Cover and refrigerate until completely cold or overnight.

5. Stir cream mixture. Transfer to an ice cream maker and freeze according to manufacturer's instructions.

**VARIATION:** *Cherry Custard Chocolate Marble Ice Cream:* *When the ice cream is semifrozen, stop the ice cream maker and scoop ice cream into a freezerproof container. Using a knife, swirl in ¼ cup (50 mL) melted dark chocolate to create marbled effect. Freeze until firm.*

# Chestnut Ice Cream

**SERVES 6 TO 8**

**Tips:** This ice cream will be soft. For firmer ice cream, place in the freezer for at least 2 hours.

Chestnut purée comes in a 1-lb 6-oz (675 mL) can. Leftovers are great as a dessert crêpe filling.

*Chestnut purée can be found in gourmet food shops and some supermarkets in the imported foods section. If the purée doesn't have vanilla added, add 1 tsp (5 mL) vanilla to the recipe before you refrigerate.*

| | | |
|---|---|---|
| 3 | egg yolks | 3 |
| 1/3 cup | granulated sugar | 75 mL |
| 1 cup | 2% milk (see Tips, page 30) | 250 mL |
| 1 cup | table (18%) cream | 250 mL |
| 1 1/4 cups | unsweetened chestnut purée with vanilla added (see Tips, left) | 300 mL |
| 1 cup | whipping (35%) cream | 250 mL |
| Pinch | salt | Pinch |

1. In a bowl, whisk egg yolks with sugar until thickened and pale yellow. Set aside.

2. In a medium saucepan over medium-low heat, bring milk and table cream to a simmer. Stir in chestnut purée. Gradually whisk into the egg mixture.

3. Return entire mixture to the saucepan. Cook over low heat, stirring constantly, until the mixture is thick enough to coat the back of a wooden spoon. Be careful not to let it boil. Strain into a clean large bowl. Let cool to room temperature.

4. Stir in whipping cream and salt. Cover and refrigerate until completely cold or overnight.

5. Stir cream mixture. Transfer to an ice cream maker and freeze according to manufacturer's instructions.

# Chocolate Hazelnut Ice Cream

**SERVES 8**

**Tip:** If you prefer just a hint of hazelnut flavor, reduce the chocolate hazelnut spread to ¹/₂ cup (125 mL).

**Serving suggestion:** Splash your scoop with your favorite hazelnut liqueur.

*Ever wondered what else you could do with chocolate hazelnut spread other than put it on toast? We melted it into ice cream and found the result delicious. This spread gives the ice cream a pleasantly grainy, slightly chewy texture.*

| | | |
|---|---|---|
| 2 cups | whipping (35%) cream | 500 mL |
| 2 cups | milk | 500 mL |
| 1 cup | chocolate hazelnut spread (see Tip, left) | 250 mL |
| ¹/₂ cup | granulated sugar | 125 mL |
| ¹/₄ cup | chopped hazelnuts | 50 mL |

1. In a medium saucepan over medium-low heat, bring cream and milk to a simmer.

2. In a large bowl, stir hazelnut spread with sugar until smooth. Whisk ¹/₄ cup (50 mL) of the cream mixture into the sugar mixture until smooth. Whisk in remaining cream mixture until blended. Cover and refrigerate until completely cold or overnight.

3. Stir cream mixture. Transfer to an ice cream maker and freeze according to manufacturer's instructions.

4. Serve sprinkled with chopped hazelnuts.

> **VARIATION:** *Double Chocolate Hazelnut Ice Cream: If you really love chocolate, add ¹/₂ cup (125 mL) chopped good-quality dark chocolate and the hazelnuts a few seconds before the ice cream churning has finished.*

# Classic Chocolate Ice Cream

**SERVES 6 TO 8**

*Everybody needs a basic recipe for chocolate ice cream, which is one of the five most popular flavors in North America. This one is simple but does the trick. A couple of scoops make the perfect dessert. To make it even more decadent, add a chocolate sauce topping or a sprinkle of chocolate nuts or chopped nuts.*

**DOUBLE BOILER**

| | | |
|---|---|---|
| 6 oz | bittersweet chocolate, coarsely chopped | 175 g |
| 1/4 cup | unsweetened cocoa powder | 50 mL |
| 4 | egg yolks | 4 |
| 3/4 cup | granulated sugar | 175 mL |
| 2 cups | whipping (35%) cream | 500 mL |
| 2 cups | milk | 500 mL |
| 1 tsp | vanilla | 5 mL |

1. In the top of a double boiler over medium heat, melt chocolate (see Tip, page 34). Gradually whisk in cocoa until smooth. Set aside.

2. In a bowl, whisk egg yolks with sugar until thickened and pale yellow. Set aside.

3. In a medium saucepan over medium-low heat, bring cream and milk to a simmer. Gradually whisk into the egg mixture.

4. Return the entire mixture to the saucepan. Cook over low heat, stirring constantly, until the mixture is thick enough to coat the back of a wooden spoon. Be careful not to let it boil. Strain into a clean large bowl. Let cool to room temperature.

5. Stir in melted chocolate and vanilla. Cover and refrigerate until completely cold or overnight.

6. Stir cream mixture. Transfer to an ice cream maker and freeze according to manufacturer's instructions.

# NEAPOLITAN ICE CREAM

*Bricks of chocolate, strawberry and vanilla ice cream are known as Neapolitan and are easy to make at home. You can layer homemade ice cream immediately after it's finished churning or you can soften already frozen homemade or store-bought ice cream, layer it, then refreeze it until it's solid.*

9-BY 5-INCH (1.5 L) LOAF PAN,
LINED WITH PLASTIC WRAP OR WAXED PAPER

| 2 cups | chocolate ice cream | 500 mL |
| 2 cups | strawberry ice cream | 500 mL |
| 2 cups | vanilla ice cream | 500 mL |

1. Soften chocolate ice cream at room temperature for 15 minutes. Spread softened ice cream in prepared pan. Smooth top with a spatula. Freeze until firm.

2. Soften strawberry ice cream at room temperature for 15 minutes. Spread softened ice cream over first layer. Smooth top with a spatula. Freeze until firm.

3. Soften vanilla ice cream at room temperature for 15 minutes. Spread softened ice cream over second layer. Smooth top with a spatula. Cover with plastic wrap or waxed paper and freeze for 4 hours or until firm.

4. To serve, unwrap and turn out of pan onto cutting board. Peel off plastic wrap. Using a warm dry knife, cut into slices or scoop into sundaes drizzled with chocolate sauce.

SERVES 6 TO 8

# Chocolate Malt Ice Cream

**SERVES 6 TO 8**

**Tip:** This ice cream will be soft. For firmer ice cream, place in the freezer for at least 2 hours.

*This very rich ice cream, reminiscent of those at a '40s malt shop, is chocolaty but not too sweet. You can find malted milk powder in most large supermarkets in the same section as hot chocolate powders.*

| 2 | eggs | 2 |
|---|------|---|
| 4 oz | unsweetened chocolate, chopped | 125 g |
| 2 cups | table (18%) cream | 500 mL |
| ¾ cup | granulated sugar | 175 mL |
| ⅓ cup | malted milk powder | 75 mL |
| 1 cup | whipping (35%) cream | 250 mL |
| 2 tsp | vanilla | 10 mL |

1. In a bowl, whisk eggs until pale yellow. Set aside.

2. In a medium saucepan, combine chocolate, table cream, sugar and malted milk powder. Cook over low heat, stirring occasionally, until chocolate is melted and sugar is dissolved. Increase heat to medium-low. Bring to a simmer. Cook, stirring constantly, for 1 minute to combine. Gradually whisk into the eggs.

3. Return entire mixture to the saucepan. Cook over low heat, stirring constantly, until the mixture is thick enough to coat the back of a wooden spoon. Be careful not to let it boil. Strain into a clean large bowl. Let cool to room temperature.

4. Stir in whipping cream and vanilla. Cover and refrigerate until completely cold or overnight.

5. Stir cream mixture. Transfer to an ice cream maker and freeze according to manufacturer's instructions.

# Chocolate Mousse Ice Cream

**SERVES 6 TO 8**

*This ice cream tastes like frozen chocolate mousse. Unlike the classic French dessert, this treat has no eggs, just loads of bittersweet chocolate. Use the best-quality chocolate you can find. It will definitely make a difference!*

| | | |
|---|---|---|
| 12 oz | bittersweet chocolate, chopped | 375 g |
| 2 cups | milk | 500 mL |
| 2 cups | whipping (35%) cream | 500 mL |
| 1/2 cup | granulated sugar | 125 mL |
| 1 tbsp | vanilla | 15 mL |

1. Place chocolate in a bowl. In a medium saucepan over medium-low heat, bring milk, cream and sugar to a simmer, stirring occasionally. Gradually whisk into chocolate until smooth. Whisk in vanilla.

2. Cover and refrigerate until completely cold or overnight.

3. Stir cream mixture. Transfer to an ice cream maker and freeze according to manufacturer's instructions.

# Cinnamon Stick
# Ice Cream

**SERVES 4 TO 6**

*Cinnamon is a key ingredient in many desserts, but this time we made it the star. Our secret is to double the cinnamon by steeping a cinnamon stick in the cream in addition to adding some of the ground variety to the custard before freezing.*

| | | |
|---|---|---|
| 3 cups | table (18%) cream | 750 mL |
| ¾ cup | granulated sugar | 175 mL |
| 1 | cinnamon stick | 1 |
| 1 tbsp | ground cinnamon | 15 mL |
| 1 tsp | vanilla | 5 mL |

1. In a medium saucepan over medium-low heat, bring cream, sugar and cinnamon stick to a simmer.

2. Strain into a clean large bowl. Whisk in ground cinnamon and vanilla. Let stand for 30 minutes.

3. Cover and refrigerate until completely cold or overnight. Remove cinnamon stick.

4. Stir cream mixture. Transfer to an ice cream maker and freeze according to manufacturer's instructions.

---

**VARIATIONS:** *Red-Hot Cinnamon Ice Cream: For a Valentine's Day treat, add ¼ cup (50 mL) red-hot heart candies in the last 5 minutes of freezing. Or sprinkle candies over each serving of Cinnamon Stick Ice Cream.*

*Cinnamon Nutmeg Ice Cream: Add 2 tsp (10 mL) ground nutmeg along with the ground cinnamon.*

# Coconut Ice Cream

**Tip:** To toast coconut, spread the coconut in a thin layer in a metal cake pan or on a rimmed baking sheet. Toast in 350°F (180°C) oven, watching carefully to prevent burning or overbrowning, for 3 to 5 minutes or until golden and fragrant. Let cool to room temperature.

**Serving suggestion:** Serve a scoop of Coconut Ice Cream on a pool of Raspberry Coulis. To make: In a blender, purée 1 cup (250 mL) semithawed frozen sweetened raspberries. Strain through a fine sieve to remove seeds. Coulis will keep covered and refrigerated for up to 1 week.

*We love the stark white color of this rich dessert, but you can add a little color by toasting the coconut flakes first. Although we call for a 15-oz (426 mL) can of coconut cream, your store may only stock 14-oz (398 mL) cans. As long as the difference in size is no more than 1 oz (30 mL), the recipe should turn out just fine. Don't confuse coconut cream, which is thick and sweetened, with coconut milk, which is thinner and unsweetened.*

| | | |
|---|---|---|
| 1 | can (15 oz/426 mL) coconut cream (see Introduction, above) | 1 |
| 1 1/2 cups | whipping (35%) cream | 375 mL |
| 1 cup | milk | 250 mL |
| 1/2 cup | sweetened flaked coconut (see Tip, left) | 125 mL |

1. In a food processor or blender, purée coconut cream, whipping cream, milk and flaked coconut until thoroughly blended.

2. Transfer to an ice cream maker and freeze according to manufacturer's instructions.

> **VARIATION:** *Thai Coconut Lemongrass Ice Cream: For a fragrant, Thai-inspired dessert, infuse the coconut with lemongrass. Cut 4 stalks lemongrass in half lengthwise. Using a mallet, meat pounder, rolling pin or hammer, pound the stalks a few times to release their flavor. In a medium saucepan, bring coconut cream and lemongrass to a boil. Remove from heat and let stand for 30 minutes. Remove lemongrass stalks and proceed with recipe.*

# Coconut Mango
# Ice Cream

**SERVES 6**

**Tip:** Puréed fresh mango can be stringy. For a smoother texture, press mango through a sieve before measuring.

*This exotic ice cream with the color of a gorgeous sunset requires no fuss to prepare. You can use fresh ripe mango or sliced mango from a can. Either way, place in a food processor or blender and purée until smooth.*

| | | |
|---|---|---|
| I | can (14 oz/398 mL) coconut cream (see Introduction, page 47) | I |
| 2 cups | puréed mango (see Tip, left) | 500 mL |
| 1/2 cup | milk | 125 mL |
| 1/2 cup | table (18%) cream | 125 mL |

1. In a bowl, stir together coconut cream, mango, milk and table cream until combined.

2. Transfer to an ice cream maker and freeze according to manufacturer's instructions.

# Cola Ice Cream

**SERVES 6**

*This is a favorite recipe of preteens, who enjoy the slushy, syrupy texture and love to experiment with different soda pops. Our favorites, though, are traditional cola and root beer.*

| | | |
|---|---|---|
| I | can (12 oz/325 mL) soda pop, preferably cola or root beer | I |
| 2 cups | 2% milk (see Tips, page 30) | 500 mL |
| I cup | half-and-half (10%) cream | 250 mL |
| ¼ cup | granulated sugar | 50 mL |

1. In a bowl, stir together pop, milk, cream and sugar.

2. Transfer to an ice cream maker and freeze according to manufacturer's instructions.

---

**VARIATIONS:** *Cherry Cola Ice Cream: Add 1 tbsp (15 mL) cherry syrup.*
*Vanilla Cola Ice Cream: Add ½ tsp (2 mL) vanilla.*

# Cookies and Cream Ice Cream

**SERVES 6 TO 8**

**Tips:** This ice cream will be soft. For firmer ice cream, place in the freezer for at least 2 hours.

Remember to add the cookies at the very end of churning or they'll get too soggy.

To simplify the preparation, use 2 tsp (10 mL) vanilla extract instead of steeping the vanilla pod in the milk. Add the vanilla right before refrigerating.

*This flavor has become so popular that even frozen yogurt places have embraced it. We find that kids and adults alike love it with chocolate sandwich cookies, but adults are more adventurous and like everything from ginger to sesame cookies crumbled in. Any cookie you dunk in a cup of milk will make a tasty addition to this dessert, which is based on an excellent basic vanilla ice cream.*

| | | |
|---|---|---|
| 3 | egg yolks | 3 |
| 6 tbsp | granulated sugar | 90 mL |
| 1 | vanilla bean (see Tips, left) | 1 |
| 1½ cups | 2% milk (see Tips, page 30) | 375 mL |
| 1½ cups | whipping (35%) cream | 375 mL |
| 1½ cups | crushed cookies, such as chocolate sandwich cookies | 375 mL |

1. In a bowl, whisk egg yolks with sugar until thickened and pale yellow. Set aside.

2. Slit vanilla bean lengthwise and scrape seeds into a medium saucepan. Add vanilla pod, milk and cream. Place saucepan over medium-low heat and bring mixture just to a simmer. Remove from heat. Let stand for 15 minutes, allowing the flavor of the vanilla to infuse.

**Serving suggestion:** For a children's party, scoop balls of ice cream onto parchment paper-lined cookie sheet. Top each with a sugar cone to make a hat and use candy to make faces. Think wizards, witches and clowns.

3. Discard pod. Bring to a simmer over medium-low heat and simmer for 5 minutes. Gradually whisk into the egg mixture.

4. Return entire mixture to the saucepan. Cook over low heat, stirring constantly, until the mixture is thick enough to coat the back of a wooden spoon. Be careful not to let it boil. Strain into a clean large bowl. Let cool to room temperature. Cover and refrigerate until completely cold or overnight.

5. Stir cream mixture. Transfer to an ice cream maker and freeze according to manufacturer's instructions.

6. Add cookies in the last 5 minutes of freezing and let machine stir them in.

> **VARIATION:** *Cake and Cream Ice Cream: You can mix in cakes and crumbs, too. For maximum crunchiness, dry them out in a 200°F (100°C) oven for 5 to 10 minutes. Let cool to room temperature. Add in the last 5 minutes of freezing.*

# Corn Ice Cream

**SERVES 6 TO 8**

**Tip:** Do not substitute fresh corn for the cream-style corn, which works best in this recipe.

*Skeptics are transformed into fans when they try this absolutely delicious treat. This unusual ice cream, with the hint of maple syrup, is a terrific topping for cornbread, gingerbread or lemon pound cake. If you prefer a smoother texture, pass the corn through a food mill before adding it to the cream mixture.*

| | | |
|---|---|---|
| 3 | egg yolks | 3 |
| ½ cup | granulated sugar | 125 mL |
| ¾ cup | pure maple syrup | 175 mL |
| I cup | half-and-half (10%) cream | 250 mL |
| I cup | whipping (35%) cream | 250 mL |
| I | can (14 oz/398 mL) cream-style corn (see Tip, left) | I |
| I tsp | vanilla | 5 mL |

1. In a bowl, whisk egg yolks with sugar until thickened and pale yellow. Whisk in maple syrup. Set aside.

2. In a medium saucepan over medium-low heat, bring half-and-half and whipping cream to a simmer. Gradually whisk into the egg mixture.

3. Return entire mixture to the saucepan. Cook over low heat, stirring constantly, until the mixture is thick enough to coat the back of a wooden spoon. Be careful not to let it boil. Strain into a clean large bowl. Let cool to room temperature.

4. Stir in corn and vanilla. Cover and refrigerate until completely cold or overnight.

5. Stir cream mixture. Transfer to an ice cream maker and freeze according to manufacturer's instructions.

# Mix-Ins

*The sky's the limit when it comes to what you can add to basic ice cream flavors such as vanilla or chocolate. You can mix in anything from crushed cookies to smashed toffee in the last 5 minutes of freezing or you can smush your signature additions into store-bought or previously frozen homemade ice cream.*

**Here's our Top 20**

- diced dried apricots
- brownie pieces
- crumbled gingersnaps
- chocolate-covered espresso beans
- toasted flaked coconut
- M&M's
- Reese's Pieces
- Grape-Nuts
- granola
- semisweet and white chocolate chips
- chopped sponge toffee
- Gummi Bears
- toasted nuts
- chocolate sprinkles
- peanuts
- raisins
- red pepper flakes
- ground cinnamon
- chopped dates
- crushed peppermint candy canes

# Crème Brûlée Ice Cream

## SERVES 6 TO 8

**Tip:** Do not leave the stove when making caramelized sugar because it can easily burn. Caramelized sugar is very hot, so be careful to avoid any contact with hands or mouth until it has cooled completely.

**Serving suggestion:** Pack ice cream into ramekins or custard cups and smooth tops. Sprinkle crackled sugar over top and serve individually like a classic crème brûlée.

*This ice cream gets its distinctive flavor from the marriage of vanilla and crackled caramelized sugar. The frozen version is just as satisfying, elegant and trendy as the real thing. Although the sugar topping enhances the ice cream, a five-year-old friend informs us that this is not a kid-friendly ice cream, because the shards can be too sharp for little mouths.*

CANDY THERMOMETER
BAKING SHEET, GREASED AND LINED WITH FOIL

### ICE CREAM

| 4 | egg yolks | 4 |
|---|---|---|
| ¾ cup | granulated sugar | 175 mL |
| I | vanilla bean | I |
| 2 cups | milk | 500 mL |
| 2 cups | whipping (35%) cream | 500 mL |

### CRACKLED CARAMELIZED SUGAR TOPPING

| ¾ cup | granulated sugar | 175 mL |
|---|---|---|
| 2 tbsp | cold water | 25 mL |
| 2 tbsp | corn syrup | 25 mL |

I. To make Ice Cream: In a bowl, whisk egg yolks with sugar until thickened and pale yellow. Set aside.

2. Slit vanilla bean lengthwise and scrape seeds into a medium saucepan. Add vanilla pod, milk and cream. Place saucepan over medium-low heat and bring milk mixture just to a simmer. Remove from heat. Let stand for 15 minutes, allowing the flavor of the vanilla to infuse.

3. Discard pod. Bring to a simmer over medium-low heat and simmer for 5 minutes. Gradually whisk into the egg mixture.

**4.** Return entire mixture to the saucepan. Cook over low heat, stirring constantly, until the mixture is thick enough to coat the back of a wooden spoon. Be careful not to let it boil. Strain into a clean large bowl. Let cool to room temperature. Cover and refrigerate until completely cold or overnight.

**5.** Stir cream mixture. Transfer to an ice cream maker and freeze according to manufacturer's instructions.

**6.** To make Crackled Caramelized Sugar Topping: In a medium saucepan, stir together sugar, water and corn syrup. Bring to a boil. Cook over medium heat, brushing down the side of the saucepan with cold water occasionally, until candy thermometer registers 300°F (150°C) or mixture turns golden brown.

**7.** Carefully pour onto prepared baking sheet. Let cool completely. Break into shards. Set aside.

**8.** When ready to serve, place two scoops of ice cream in a bowl and top with crackled sugar.

> **VARIATION:** *Crème Caramel Ice Cream: To make caramel sauce, increase water in Crackled Caramelized Sugar Topping to ¼ cup (50 mL). Once sugar mixture is golden brown, stir in 1½ cups (375 mL) whipping (35%) cream until foaming subsides. Be very cautious when adding the whipping cream (the mixture will foam and splatter). Hold the saucepan at arm's length and avert your face when adding the cream. To serve, pour caramel sauce over ice cream.*

# Dulce de Leche Ice Cream

## SERVES 4

**Tips:** For soft ice cream, serve immediately. Or freeze overnight until firm.

If cinnamon is not your thing, it's just as delicious without it.

**Serving suggestion:** Line each cup of a muffin tin with plastic wrap. Pack with ice cream and freeze. Turn the individual portions out onto plates, drizzle with chocolate sauce and sprinkle with unsweetened cocoa powder.

*Dulce de leche, a traditional Latin American topping, has found a place on many desserts, such as this ice cream. It's not just fun to eat but also fun to make because it's so easy — all you have to do is stir the sweetened condensed milk. You won't believe that the caramel is made from that one simple ingredient.*

| | | |
|---|---|---|
| 1 | can (10 oz/300 mL) sweetened condensed milk | 1 |
| 1 cup | whipping (35%) cream | 250 mL |
| 1 cup | milk | 250 mL |
| 1 | cinnamon stick (see Tips, left) | 1 |
| 2 tsp | vanilla | 10 mL |

1. In a medium saucepan over medium heat, cook condensed milk, stirring constantly, until thick and golden brown, about 15 minutes. Remove from heat.

2. Meanwhile, in a separate medium saucepan over medium-low heat, bring cream, milk and cinnamon stick to a simmer. Remove cinnamon stick.

3. Very slowly and carefully to prevent spattering, pour condensed milk into a clean large bowl. Gradually whisk in cream mixture, holding the saucepan at arm's length and averting your face when adding the cream. Whisk in vanilla. Cover and refrigerate until completely cold or overnight.

4. Stir cream mixture. Transfer to an ice cream maker and freeze according to manufacturer's instructions.

> **VARIATION:** *Traditional Dulce de Leche: If you're not in an ice cream mood, do as they do in Latin American countries: cook the sweetened condensed milk down into dulce de leche and, instead of freezing it into ice cream, spread it on toast or your favorite pound cake.*

# Eggnog Ice Cream

**SERVES 8 TO 10**

**Tips:** We used 2 tbsp (25 mL) rum extract because we like flavors exaggerated. If you don't prefer such a strong rum flavor, feel free to reduce the extract to 1 tbsp (15 mL).

Do not use too much alcohol; if you do, you'll have a hard time getting your ice cream to freeze.

*This perfect ice cream for the holidays can be made with store-bought eggnog, as in the Variation (below), or by following this traditional recipe for an egg-custard base. It can be tricky to find a carton of store-bought eggnog in July, but this recipe means you can make this treat all year-round.*

| 8 | egg yolks | 8 |
|---|---|---|
| 1 1/4 cups | granulated sugar | 300 mL |
| 3 cups | milk | 750 mL |
| 1 cup | whipping (35%) cream | 250 mL |
| 2 tbsp | rum extract or rum (see Tips, left) | 25 mL |
| 1 tbsp | vanilla | 15 mL |
| 1 tsp | brandy | 5 mL |
| 1/4 tsp | ground nutmeg | 1 mL |
| 1/4 tsp | ground cinnamon | 1 mL |

1. In a bowl, whisk egg yolks with sugar until thickened and pale yellow. Set aside.

2. In a medium saucepan over medium-low heat, bring milk and cream to a simmer. Gradually whisk into the egg mixture.

3. Return entire mixture to the saucepan. Cook over low heat, stirring constantly, until the mixture is thick enough to coat the back of a wooden spoon. Be careful not to let it boil. Strain into a clean large bowl. Let cool to room temperature.

4. Stir in rum extract, vanilla, brandy, nutmeg and cinnamon until thoroughly blended. Cover and refrigerate until completely cold or overnight.

5. Stir cream mixture. Transfer to an ice cream maker and freeze according to manufacturer's instructions.

**VARIATION:** *Quick Eggnog Ice Cream: To make ice cream from store-bought eggnog, omit egg yolks, sugar, milk, cream and vanilla. In a bowl, stir together 4 cups (1 L) store-bought eggnog, rum extract, brandy, nutmeg and cinnamon. Transfer to an ice cream maker and freeze according to manufacturer's instructions.*

# Fig Chutney Ice Cream

**SERVES 4 TO 6**

**Serving suggestion:**
Serve with sliced
fresh mangoes.

*Plump dried figs give a more satisfying and intense flavor to this ice cream than do fresh figs. Enjoy this as an ending to a meal of simply prepared grilled meat, such as barbecued lamb.*

| | | |
|---|---|---|
| I | large banana, sliced | I |
| 6 | dried figs, finely chopped | 6 |
| ½ cup | Simple Syrup (see recipe, page 23) | 125 mL |
| I cup | whipping (35%) cream | 250 mL |
| I cup | milk | 250 mL |
| I tsp | mango chutney | 5 mL |
| ¼ tsp | vanilla | I mL |

1. In a food processor or blender, purée banana, figs and syrup until smooth.

2. Transfer to a large bowl. Stir in cream, milk, chutney and vanilla.

3. Transfer to an ice cream maker and freeze according to manufacturer's instructions.

# Ginger Ice Cream

## SERVES 6

**Tip:** Crystallized or candied ginger has already been cooked in a sugar syrup and coated with coarse sugar. If you want to add more sweet heat to the ice cream, you can increase the amount to I cup (250 mL).

**Serving suggestion:** In a food processor or blender, purée I mango, pitted and peeled, with ¼ cup (50 mL) of additional crystallized ginger. Spoon over Ginger Ice Cream or vanilla ice cream and serve.

*Ginger is a fiery, feisty spice that adds a refreshing kick to this vanilla-based ice cream. It's great plain, drizzled with chocolate sauce or topped with fruit salad.*

| | | |
|---|---|---|
| 4 | egg yolks | 4 |
| ¾ cup | granulated sugar | 175 mL |
| 2 cups | whipping (35%) cream | 500 mL |
| 2 cups | milk | 500 mL |
| ¾ cup | crystallized ginger, finely chopped (see Tip, left) | 175 mL |
| ¼ tsp | vanilla | I mL |

1. In a bowl, whisk egg yolks with sugar until thickened and pale yellow. Set aside.

2. In a medium saucepan over medium-low heat, bring cream, milk and ginger to a simmer. Gradually whisk into the egg mixture.

3. Return entire mixture to the saucepan. Cook over low heat, stirring constantly, until the mixture is thick enough to coat the back of a wooden spoon. Be careful not to let it boil. Strain into a clean large bowl. Let cool to room temperature.

4. Stir in vanilla. Cover and refrigerate until completely cold or overnight.

5. Stir cream mixture. Transfer to an ice cream maker and freeze according to manufacturer's instructions.

**VARIATION:** *Chocolate Ginger Ice Cream: Add 12 oz (375 g) bittersweet chocolate to hot cream mixture and proceed with the recipe.*

# Ginger Molasses Ice Cream

**SERVES 4 TO 6**

*Molasses, once a household staple, will become a favorite ingredient once you try this special recipe. For a festive ice cream sandwich, squish a scoop of this ice cream between two gingersnap cookies.*

| | | |
|---|---|---|
| 3 | eggs | 3 |
| 1/2 cup | granulated sugar | 125 mL |
| 1 1/2 cups | whipping (35%) cream | 375 mL |
| 1 cup | milk | 250 mL |
| 1/3 cup | fancy molasses | 75 mL |
| 1/4 cup | finely chopped crystallized ginger | 50 mL |
| 1/2 tsp | vanilla | 2 mL |

1. In a bowl, whisk eggs with sugar until thickened and pale yellow. Set aside.

2. In a medium saucepan over medium-low heat, bring cream and milk to a simmer. Gradually whisk into the egg mixture.

3. Return entire mixture to the saucepan. Cook over low heat, stirring constantly, until the mixture is thick enough to coat the back of a wooden spoon. Be careful not to let it boil. Strain into a clean large bowl. Let cool to room temperature.

4. Stir in molasses, ginger and vanilla. Cover and refrigerate until completely cold or overnight.

5. Stir cream mixture. Transfer to an ice cream maker and freeze according to manufacturer's instructions.

# Green Tea Ice Cream

*With Asian menus so popular these days, this dessert has begun to pop up everywhere. It's a terrific ending after sushi or stir-fries.*

**SERVES 4 TO 6**

| | | |
|---|---|---|
| 2 cups | milk | 500 mL |
| I cup | whipping (35%) cream | 250 mL |
| 3 tbsp | green tea leaves or green tea with mint | 45 mL |
| 2 | egg yolks | 2 |
| ¾ cup | granulated sugar | 175 mL |
| I tbsp | cornstarch | 15 mL |

1. In a medium saucepan over medium-low heat, bring milk and cream to a simmer. Remove from heat. Stir in green tea leaves and let stand for 10 minutes.

2. In a bowl, whisk egg yolks with sugar until thickened and pale yellow. Whisk in cornstarch. Gradually whisk in cream mixture.

3. Return entire mixture to the saucepan. Cook over low heat, stirring constantly, until the mixture is thick enough to coat the back of a wooden spoon. Be careful not to let it boil. Strain into a clean large bowl. Let cool to room temperature. Cover and refrigerate until completely cold or overnight.

4. Stir cream mixture. Transfer to an ice cream maker and freeze according to manufacturer's instructions.

# Guinness Ice Cream

**SERVES 4 TO 6**

*This has the slight bitterness of a good pint of stout and is absolutely delicious with a fruit crumble or Irish soda bread pudding. It provides good conversation value as well as taste.*

**Tip:** This ice cream will be soft. For firmer ice cream, place in the freezer for at least 2 hours.

| | | |
|---|---|---|
| 2 | egg yolks | 2 |
| ¾ cup | granulated sugar | 175 mL |
| 3 cups | Guinness Draft, about 1½ cans | 750 mL |
| ½ cup | milk | 125 mL |
| 1 cup | whipping (35%) cream | 250 mL |

1. In a bowl, whisk egg yolks with sugar until thickened and pale yellow. Set aside.

2. In a medium saucepan over medium heat, cook Guinness, stirring occasionally, until reduced by half. Reduce heat to low. Stir in milk. Bring to a simmer. Gradually whisk into the egg mixture.

3. Return entire mixture to the saucepan. Cook over low heat, stirring constantly, until the mixture is thick enough to coat the back of a wooden spoon. Be careful not to let it boil. Strain into a clean large bowl. Let cool to room temperature.

4. Stir in cream. Cover and refrigerate until completely cold or overnight.

5. Stir cream mixture. Transfer to an ice cream maker and freeze according to manufacturer's instructions.

# Hazelnut Honey Ice Cream

**Serving suggestion:**
Drizzle a little more orange-blossom honey over each serving.

*Toasting the hazelnuts enhances their flavor in this delectable, rich dessert. Use clover or orange-blossom honey for optimum flavor.*

| | | |
|---|---|---|
| I cup | hazelnuts | 250 mL |
| 4 | egg yolks | 4 |
| $1/3$ cup | liquid honey | 75 mL |
| $1/2$ | vanilla bean | $1/2$ |
| I cup | milk | 250 mL |
| $1/2$ cup | whipping (35%) cream | 125 mL |

1. Spread hazelnuts on rimmed baking sheet. Toast in a 350°F (180°C) oven, watching carefully to prevent burning or overbrowning, for about 5 minutes or until fragrant. Transfer to two clean dish towels and rub until the skins slip off. Chop finely and set aside.

2. In a bowl, whisk egg yolks with honey until thickened and pale yellow. Set aside.

3. Slit vanilla bean lengthwise and scrape seeds into a medium saucepan. Add vanilla pod, milk and cream. Place saucepan over medium-low heat and bring just to a simmer. Remove from heat. Let stand for 15 minutes, allowing the flavor of the vanilla to infuse.

4. Discard pod. Bring to a simmer over medium-low heat and simmer for 5 minutes. Gradually whisk into the egg mixture.

5. Return entire mixture to the saucepan. Cook over low heat, stirring constantly, until the mixture is thick enough to coat the back of a wooden spoon. Be careful not to let it boil. Let cool to room temperature. Cover and refrigerate until completely cold or overnight.

6. Transfer to an ice cream maker and freeze according to manufacturer's instructions. Add hazelnuts in the last 5 minutes of freezing and let machine stir them in.

# Honey Vanilla Ice Cream

**SERVES 4**

**Tip:** For extra richness, substitute the seeds from one vanilla bean for the vanilla extract. Slit vanilla bean lengthwise. Scrape seeds into a medium saucepan. Add vanilla pod, milk and cream. Bring to a simmer over medium-low heat. Proceed with recipe.

*This was a favorite among our taste testers. It's especially enjoyable as is, but also makes a wonderful base for all sorts of additions, from crushed peanuts to chocolate chips to toasted coconut to chopped dates.*

| | | |
|---|---|---|
| 4 | egg yolks | 4 |
| $^1/_2$ cup | liquid honey | 125 mL |
| I cup | whipping (35%) cream | 250 mL |
| I cup | milk | 250 mL |
| I tbsp | vanilla | 15 mL |

1. In a bowl, whisk egg yolks with honey until thickened and pale yellow. Set aside.

2. In a medium saucepan over medium-low heat, bring cream and milk to a simmer. Gradually whisk into the egg mixture.

3. Return entire mixture to the saucepan. Cook over low heat, stirring constantly, until the mixture is thick enough to coat the back of a wooden spoon. Be careful not to let it boil. Strain into a clean large bowl. Let cool to room temperature.

4. Stir in vanilla. Cover and refrigerate until completely cold or overnight.

5. Transfer to an ice cream maker and freeze according to manufacturer's instructions.

Green Tea Ice Cream (page 61)
*Overleaf:* Neapolitan Ice Cream Sundaes (page 43)

**VARIATIONS:** *Lavender Vanilla Ice Cream:* *This delicious treat is found throughout the south of France, where the flowering herb grows in every garden and at the sides of roads. Add 2 tbsp (25 mL) crushed dried lavender flowers to the strained cream mixture. When you buy lavender, do not buy the kind used in potpourri. If you buy it from an herb grower, it's certainly safe to eat.*

*Prune Armagnac Ice Cream:* *With added nuggets of brandy-macerated prunes, this ice cream becomes even more exquisite. In a bowl, pour ¼ cup (50 mL) Armagnac, brandy or port over 1 cup (250 mL) chopped prunes. Refrigerate overnight, tossing once or twice to ensure that prunes are coated with Armagnac. Add to ice cream maker in the last 5 minutes of freezing and let machine stir them in.*

*Honey Vanilla Ice Cream with Strawberry Jam Ripple:* *A dramatic effect and surprisingly simple to do, rippling or marbling enhances flavor and provides color contrast. There are two methods for creating ribbons of flavor. The second method works well for puréed raspberries and chocolate sauce. For best results, choose marbling colors that are markedly different from that of the ice cream.*

*1. Remove Honey Vanilla Ice Cream from the machine when it is semisoft and transfer to a freezerproof container. Using a knife or fork, gently swirl 1 tbsp (15 mL) softly set strawberry jam into the ice cream. Cover and freeze until firm.*

*2. Remove Honey Vanilla Ice Cream from the machine when it is semisoft. Alternately spoon layers of ice cream and softly set jam into a freezerproof container. Make about three layers. Using a knife, gently swirl a couple of times. Cover and freeze until firm.*

Peppermint Chocolate Chip Ice Cream (page 87)

# Kids' Cooler

**SERVES 2**

*On a hot summer day, kids will welcome this ice cream craft. It won't result in premium-quality ice cream, but it's a fun idea and it beautifully demonstrates the old-fashioned ice-and-salt method of making ice cream.*

1 SANDWICH-SIZE RESEALABLE PLASTIC BAG
1 LARGE-SIZE RESEALABLE PLASTIC FREEZER BAG

| | | |
|---|---|---|
| ¾ cup | half-and-half (10%) cream | 175 mL |
| 1 tbsp | granulated sugar | 15 mL |
| 1 tbsp | chocolate syrup | 15 mL |
| ½ tsp | vanilla | 2 mL |
| | Ice cubes | |
| 6 tbsp | rock salt | 90 mL |

1. In the sandwich-size bag, combine cream, sugar, chocolate syrup and vanilla. Seal bag.

2. Fill large-size plastic bag halfway with ice cubes. Add rock salt, then sandwich-size bag. Seal bag.

3. Shake bags vigorously for 8 to 10 minutes or until thickened and mixture turns into ice cream.

# Key Lime
# Ice Cream

**SERVES 4**

*A popular, and less fussy, method of making ice cream is to use condensed milk as the base. In this version, the fat of traditional ice cream is substantially reduced (thanks to the partly skimmed condensed milk) without sacrificing taste. Use bottled key lime juice (now available at many gourmet grocery stores) rather than juice from traditional limes.*

| | | |
|---|---|---|
| I | can (10 oz/300 mL) sweetened condensed partly skimmed milk | I |
| I cup | Simple Syrup (see recipe, page 23) | 250 mL |
| ½ cup | key lime juice | 125 mL |

**1.** In a bowl, stir together condensed milk, syrup and lime juice.

**2.** Transfer to an ice cream maker and freeze according to manufacturer's instructions.

---

**VARIATIONS:** *Tart Key Lime Ice Cream:* Reduce Simple Syrup to ½ cup (125 mL).

*Margarita Ice Cream:* Add 2 tbsp (25 mL) each tequila and orange-flavored liqueur to the machine in the last 5 minutes of freezing and let machine stir them in.

---

# Key Lime Pie Ice Cream

*Fans of the popular Florida dessert will want to try this because it's tart and creamy with a graham cracker crust blended right in.*

**SERVES 4 TO 6**

| | | |
|---|---|---|
| 3 | eggs | 3 |
| I cup | granulated sugar | 250 mL |
| I cup | whipping (35%) cream | 250 mL |
| ½ cup | milk | 125 mL |
| ½ cup | key lime juice | 125 mL |
| ½ cup | mini-marshmallows | 125 mL |
| 3 | graham crackers, broken into small pieces | 3 |

1. In a bowl, whisk eggs with sugar until thickened and pale yellow. Set aside.

2. In a medium saucepan over medium-low heat, bring cream and milk to a simmer. Gradually whisk into the egg mixture.

3. Return entire mixture to the saucepan. Cook over low heat, stirring constantly, until the mixture is thick enough to coat the back of a wooden spoon. Be careful not to let it boil. Strain into a clean large bowl. Let cool to room temperature.

4. Stir in lime juice. Cover and refrigerate until completely cold or overnight.

5. Transfer to an ice cream maker and freeze according to manufacturer's instructions.

6. Add marshmallows and graham crackers in the last 5 minutes of freezing and let machine stir them in.

# Kulfi

*There are many variations of this sticky ice cream that is popular in Indian cultures; some even call for the addition of white bread as a thickening agent. Ours is adapted from a recipe by our friend Rosemarie DeSouza, who says that it's tried-and-true and enjoyed by her family members both here and in Goa. Unlike traditional North American ice cream, this one is made using the freezer method and not a machine.*

KULFI MOLDS, MUFFIN TIN OR
8-INCH (2 L) SQUARE BAKING PAN OR DISH,
LINED WITH PLASTIC WRAP

| | | |
|---|---|---|
| I | can (10 oz/300 mL) sweetened condensed partly skimmed milk | I |
| I | can (14 oz/385 mL) evaporated skim milk | I |
| I cup | light (5%) cream | 250 mL |
| 2 tsp | ground cardamom | 10 mL |
| I tsp | vanilla | 5 mL |
| I cup | pistachios, chopped or whole | 250 mL |

1. In a large bowl, stir together condensed milk, evaporated milk and cream. Stir in cardamom and vanilla.

2. Pour into kulfi molds, muffin tins or prepared baking pan. Cover with plastic wrap.

3. Freeze for at least 6 hours or overnight. Turn out of molds or muffins cups onto serving plates or scoop out of the square pan or cut into cubes. Serve sprinkled with pistachios.

---

**VARIATION:** *Saffron Pistachio Kulfi:* Add $1/2$ tsp (2 mL) *saffron threads and* $1/2$ *cup (125 mL) chopped pistachios to the mixture before pouring into molds. Garnish with* $1/2$ *cup (125 mL) chopped pistachios.*

# Lemon Ice Cream

**SERVES 6**

**Serving suggestion:**
You will need an additional 6 lemons. Use these lemons as shells for the ice cream: Cut one-third off the top of each lemon. Set tops aside. Squeeze juice out of the bottoms, then scrape out any membranes. Scoop ice cream into shells. Top with lids. Freeze until ready to serve.

*We like this at its most lemony, but you can cut back on the lemon if you prefer just a hint of citrus. This ice cream provides a wonderful background on which to explore different taste sensations (see Variations, below).*

| 4 | egg yolks | 4 |
| | Zest and juice of 2 lemons | |
| 2 cups | whipping (35%) cream | 500 mL |
| 1 cup | milk | 250 mL |
| 2/3 cup | granulated sugar | 150 mL |

**1.** In a bowl, whisk egg yolks with lemon zest until pale yellow. Set aside.

**2.** In a medium saucepan over medium-low heat, bring cream, milk and sugar to a simmer, stirring constantly, until sugar is dissolved.

**3.** Gradually whisk into the egg mixture.

**4.** Return entire mixture to the saucepan. Cook over low heat, stirring constantly, until the mixture is thick enough to coat the back of a wooden spoon. Be careful not to let it boil. Strain into a clean large bowl. Let cool to room temperature.

**5.** Stir in lemon juice. Cover and refrigerate until completely cold or overnight.

**6.** Transfer to an ice cream maker and freeze according to manufacturer's instructions.

**VARIATIONS:** *Add 1/4 cup (50 mL) poppy seeds for a crunchy texture or 1/4 cup (50 mL) mini-marshmallows for a mellow flavor. Another variation, inspired by a Danish friend's lemon pepper cookies, is to add 1 tbsp (15 mL) freshly ground black pepper. Add in the last 5 minutes of freezing and let machine stir them in.*

# THREE-LAYERED ICE CREAM TERRINE

*For a special party, make a three-layered ice cream terrine using Ginger Molasses Ice Cream, Lemon Ice Cream and Pear Cardamom Sorbet.*

9-BY 5-INCH (1.5 L) LOAF PAN,
LINED WITH PLASTIC WRAP OR WAXED PAPER

| | | |
|---|---|---|
| 2 cups | Ginger Molasses Ice Cream (see recipe, page 60) | 500 mL |
| 2 cups | Lemon Ice Cream (see recipe, page 70) | 500 mL |
| 2 cups | Pear Cardamom Sorbet (see recipe, page 138) | 500 mL |

1. Soften Ginger Molasses Ice Cream at room temperature for 15 minutes. Spread softened ice cream in prepared pan. Smooth top with a spatula. Freeze until firm.

2. Soften Lemon Ice Cream at room temperature for 15 minutes. Spread over first layer. Smooth top with a spatula. Freeze until firm.

3. Soften Pear Cardamom Sorbet at room temperature for 15 minutes. Spread over second layer. Smooth top with a spatula. Cover with plastic wrap or waxed paper and freeze for 4 hours or until firm.

4. To serve, unwrap and turn out of pan onto cutting board. Peel off plastic wrap. Using a warm dry knife, cut into slices.

SERVES 6 TO 8

# Mango-Mascarpone Ice Cream

**SERVES 4**

**Serving suggestion:**
You can easily make a party-size ice cream cake at home. Slice one store-bought loaf cake (preferably a 9-by 5-inch/1.5 L lemon pound cake) horizontally into thirds. Line a 9-by 5-inch (1.5 L) loaf pan with plastic wrap. Place the bottom cake layer in the pan. Spread layer of softened ice cream ½ inch (1 cm) deep over top. Repeat layers once. Top with remaining cake layer. Wrap with plastic wrap and freeze until firm. A few minutes before serving, cut into 2-inch (5 cm) slices. Serve with fresh fruit or Raspberry Coulis (see recipe, page 47).

*This easy-to-make, easy-to-like ice cream combines a mild, soft Italian cheese with tropical fruit. The banana gives it a special smoothness. For a slightly lighter version, substitute whole milk for the whipping cream.*

| | | |
|---|---|---|
| I | mango, peeled and cut into chunks (about 1 ½ cups/375 mL) | I |
| I | large ripe banana, sliced | I |
| ½ cup | Simple Syrup (see recipe, page 23) | 125 mL |
| ½ cup | mascarpone cheese | 125 mL |
| ½ cup | whipping (35%) cream | 125 mL |
| I tbsp | lime zest | 15 mL |
| I tbsp | freshly squeezed lime juice | 15 mL |

1. In a food processor or blender, purée mango, banana, syrup and mascarpone cheese until smooth.

2. Transfer to a bowl. Stir in cream and lime zest and juice.

3. Transfer to an ice cream maker and freeze according to manufacturer's instructions.

> **VARIATION:** *Fudgy Mango-Mascarpone Ice Cream: Because mango and chocolate are an unbeatable combo, try combining the two. Add ½ cup (125 mL) chopped chocolate fudge in the last 5 minutes of freezing and let machine stir it in.*

# Mango-Sour Cream Ice Cream

**SERVES 6**

**Tip:** This ice cream will be soft. For firmer ice cream, place in the freezer for at least 2 hours.

*For a very easy and very good dessert, this can't be beat. The beautiful orange color looks as good as the dessert tastes. For a more intense flavor, add one more mango.*

| | | |
|---|---|---|
| 1 | mango, peeled and chopped (about 1 1/2 cups/375 mL) | 1 |
| | Juice of 1 lime | |
| 3/4 cup | granulated sugar | 175 mL |
| 1 1/2 cups | sour cream | 375 mL |

1. In a food processor or blender, purée mango, lime juice and sugar until smooth.

2. Transfer to a bowl. Stir in sour cream. Cover and refrigerate until completely cold or overnight.

3. Transfer to an ice cream maker and freeze according to manufacturer's instructions.

# Maple Walnut Ice Cream

**SERVES 4 TO 6**

This delicious ice cream owes its unique flavor to toasted walnuts and pure maple syrup. Despite the hundreds of fancy ice cream combinations now available, maple walnut is still a top seller.

**Tip:** Don't cook your egg mixture over too high a heat or the eggs will scramble. If they do scramble, strain the mixture through a fine sieve.

**Serving suggestion:** For brunch, serve a scoop of Maple Walnut Ice Cream on toasted waffles with a side of bacon and sliced fresh oranges.

| | | |
|---|---|---|
| 4 | egg yolks | 4 |
| 2/3 cup | pure maple syrup | 150 mL |
| 1 tsp | all-purpose flour | 5 mL |
| 1/4 tsp | salt | 1 mL |
| 1 cup | table (18%) cream | 250 mL |
| 1 cup | milk | 250 mL |
| 1/2 tsp | vanilla | 2 mL |
| 1/2 cup | chopped toasted walnuts (see Tip, page 37) | 125 mL |

1. In a bowl, whisk together egg yolks, maple syrup, flour and salt until combined. Set aside.

2. In a medium saucepan over medium-low heat, bring cream and milk to a simmer. Gradually whisk into the egg mixture.

3. Return entire mixture to the saucepan. Cook over low heat, stirring constantly, until the mixture is thick enough to coat the back of a wooden spoon. Be careful not to let it boil. Strain into a clean large bowl. Cool to room temperature.

4. Stir in vanilla. Cover and refrigerate until completely cold or overnight.

5. Transfer to an ice cream maker and freeze according to manufacturer's instructions. Add walnuts in the last 5 minutes of freezing and let machine stir them in.

**VARIATION:** *Caramelized Maple Walnut Ice Cream: Instead of toasting the walnuts, you can caramelize them. In a skillet over medium-high heat, melt 2 tbsp (25 mL) unsalted butter. Sauté walnuts until golden. Add 2 tbsp (25 mL) packed brown sugar. Cook, stirring, until golden brown and nuts are well coated. Let cool completely. Add to ice cream in the last 5 minutes of freezing.*

# Masala Chai Ice Cream

*If you love chai tea, the spiced Indian beverage that has become so popular, you'll enjoy this frozen version.*

## SERVES 4 TO 6

**Tip:** To crush spices, you could also use a coffee grinder or blender, but this would simply chop them up, rather than releasing the essence of the spices as the mortar and pestle does.

**Serving suggestion:** Serve with a plate of ginger cookies.

MORTAR AND PESTLE

| | | |
|---|---|---|
| ½ | cinnamon stick | ½ |
| 8 | black peppercorns | 8 |
| 6 | whole cloves | 6 |
| 3 | cardamom pods | 3 |
| 2 cups | water | 500 mL |
| 3 | slices gingerroot (each ¼ inch/0.5 cm thick) | 3 |
| ½ cup | milk | 125 mL |
| 1 cup | Simple Syrup (see recipe, page 23) | 250 mL |
| ½ cup | whipping (35%) cream | 125 mL |

1. Using a mortar and pestle, crush cinnamon, peppercorns, cloves and cardamom until fine and powdery (see Tip, left).

2. In a medium saucepan over medium-high heat, bring peppercorn mixture, water, ginger and milk to a boil. Remove from heat. Cover and let stand for 10 minutes. Strain into a clean large bowl. Let cool to room temperature.

3. Stir in syrup and cream. Cover and refrigerate until completely cold or overnight.

4. Stir cream mixture. Transfer to an ice cream maker and freeze according to manufacturer's instructions.

# Nut Brittle
# Ice Cream

*A yummy variety of nuts goes into this praline, which is best added at the very end of the ice cream maker's work.*

## SERVES 6 TO 8

**Tips:** This ice cream will be soft. For firmer ice cream, place in the freezer for at least 2 hours.

To toast hazelnuts, place on a baking sheet in 300°F (150°C) oven until just toasted. When cool, rub toasted hazelnuts in a clean dish towel to remove skins.

| | | |
|---|---|---|
| 3 | egg yolks | 3 |
| I cup | granulated sugar, divided | 250 mL |
| I 1/2 cups | 2% milk (see Tips, page 30) | 375 mL |
| I tbsp | vegetable oil | 15 mL |
| 1/2 cup | macadamia nuts, broken into halves | 125 mL |
| 1/2 cup | hazelnuts, toasted, skinned and chopped (see Tips, left) | 125 mL |
| 1/2 cup | sliced almonds | 125 mL |
| I 1/2 cups | whipping (35%) cream | 375 mL |
| 2 tsp | vanilla | 10 mL |

1. In a bowl, whisk egg yolks with 6 tbsp (90 mL) sugar until thickened and pale yellow. Set aside.

2. In a medium saucepan over medium-low heat, bring milk to a simmer. Gradually whisk into the egg mixture.

3. Return entire mixture to the saucepan. Cook over low heat, stirring constantly, until the mixture is thick enough to coat the back of a wooden spoon. Be careful not to let it boil. Strain into a clean large bowl. Let cool to room temperature.

4. Meanwhile, brush a baking sheet with vegetable oil. In a medium saucepan over medium-low heat, stir together remaining sugar, macadamia nuts, hazelnuts, almonds and ¼ cup (50 mL) water. Cook, without stirring, until sugar is dissolved. Increase heat to medium-high and boil for 3 to 5 minutes or until sugar turns golden brown and syrupy. Working quickly, pour and spread onto prepared baking sheet. Let cool until hard.

5. Stir whipping cream and vanilla into milk mixture. Cover and refrigerate until completely cold or overnight.

6. Stir cream mixture. Transfer to an ice cream maker and freeze according to manufacturer's instructions.

7. Smash about three-quarters of the nut brittle into bite-size pieces. Add in the last 5 minutes of freezing and let machine stir them in.

8. Garnish each serving with some of the remaining nut brittle.

# Oatmeal Ice Cream

**SERVES 6 TO 8**

**Tip:** This ice cream will be soft. For firmer ice cream, place in the freezer for at least 2 hours.

*Who would have thought that an ordinary breakfast cereal could make such a wonderful frozen dessert? Serving ideas are endless for this perfect brunch treat, including sliced bananas, pancakes or fresh berries. Or scoop out half a cantaloupe and fill with a scoop of Oatmeal Ice Cream, then sprinkle with granola. For dessert, serve a scoop on Baked Apples (see recipe, right). Use old-fashioned rolled oats, not instant oatmeal or quick-cooking rolled oats.*

| 3 | egg yolks | 3 |
|---|---|---|
| ¾ cup | granulated sugar | 175 mL |
| I cup | 2% milk (see Tips, page 30) | 250 mL |
| I cup | half-and-half (10%) cream | 250 mL |
| ½ cup | old-fashioned rolled oats | 125 mL |
| ½ tsp | salt | 2 mL |
| ½ tsp | ground cinnamon | 2 mL |
| I ½ cups | whipping (35%) cream | 375 mL |
| ½ cup | pure maple syrup | 125 mL |

1. In a bowl, whisk egg yolks with sugar until thickened and pale yellow. Set aside.

2. In a medium saucepan over medium heat, bring milk and half-and-half to a simmer. Add oats, salt and cinnamon. Cook, stirring constantly, for 10 minutes or until thick and creamy. Gradually whisk into the egg mixture.

3. Let cool for 15 minutes. Stir in whipping cream and maple syrup. Cover and refrigerate until completely cold or overnight.

4. Stir cream mixture. Transfer to an ice cream maker and freeze according to manufacturer's instructions.

# BAKED APPLES

*For a great comfort-food dessert, serve these baked apples warm with a scoop of Oatmeal Ice Cream (see recipe, left) and drizzle with pure maple syrup.*

PREHEAT OVEN TO 375°F (190°C)
8-INCH (2 L) SQUARE GLASS BAKING DISH

| 6 | medium cooking apples | 6 |
|---|---|---|
| 1 cup | packed brown sugar | 250 mL |
| 1/2 cup | golden raisins | 125 mL |
| 1/4 cup | unsalted butter, cut into cubes | 50 mL |
| 1/4 cup | water | 50 mL |

1. Using a potato peeler, peel the top one-third of each apple. Core, leaving bottoms intact.

2. Cut horizontally through the skin around the middle of each apple to prevent it from splitting as it cooks.

3. In a small bowl, combine brown sugar, raisins and butter until crumbly. Dividing mixture evenly among apples, spoon into cavities.

4. Place stuffed apples in baking dish. Sprinkle water in the pan. Bake in preheated oven for 30 minutes or until apples are soft and topping is bubbly.

SERVES 6

# Old-Fashioned Vanilla Ice Cream

**SERVES 6 TO 8**

**Serving suggestion:**
Ice Cream
Sandwiches:
Sandwich one
generous scoop
of softened
Old-Fashioned
Vanilla Ice Cream
between two
chocolate-covered
digestive cookies.
Gently press to
squish ice cream
to the edges of the
cookies. Using a
knife, smooth sides.
To decorate, spread
chocolate sprinkles,
toasted coconut,
mini chocolate chips
or crushed nuts on
a flat plate. Firmly
press the edges of
the sandwich into
the topping. Place
on a baking sheet
and freeze until firm.

*Any ice cream book just has to contain a recipe for vanilla ice cream,
which, though basic, is a favorite and therefore never ordinary. It really
doesn't get much better than this.*

| 4 | egg yolks | 4 |
| 3/4 cup | granulated sugar | 175 mL |
| 1 | vanilla bean | 1 |
| 2 cups | milk | 500 mL |
| 2 cups | whipping (35%) cream | 500 mL |

**1.** In a bowl, whisk egg yolks with sugar until thickened
and pale yellow. Set aside.

**2.** Slit vanilla bean lengthwise and scrape seeds into a
medium saucepan. Add vanilla pod, milk and cream.
Place saucepan over medium-low heat and bring to a
simmer. Remove from heat. Let stand for 15 minutes,
allowing the flavor of the vanilla to infuse.

**3.** Discard pod. Bring to a simmer over low heat and
simmer for 5 minutes. Gradually whisk into the egg
mixture.

**4.** Return entire mixture to the saucepan. Cook over
low heat, stirring constantly, until the mixture is thick
enough to coat the back of a wooden spoon. Be careful
not to let it boil. Strain into a clean large bowl. Let cool
to room temperature. Cover and refrigerate until
completely cold or overnight.

**5.** Transfer to an ice cream maker and freeze according to
manufacturer's instructions.

> **VARIATION:** *Saffron Ice Cream: Stir a pinch of saffron
> threads into the strained cream mixture before refrigerating.*

# BAKED ALASKA

*Transform Old-Fashioned Vanilla Ice Cream into individual servings of baked Alaska for a special party. Make sure the ice cream is very firm before slathering on the meringue. The egg whites are not fully cooked; because of today's concern over salmonella, we prefer to substitute pasteurized powdered egg whites or egg whites in a carton for fresh.*

PREHEAT OVEN TO 450°F (230°C)
BAKING SHEET, LINED WITH PARCHMENT PAPER

| | | |
|---|---|---|
| 6 | flat cookies, about 2 inches (5 cm) in diameter | 6 |
| 6 | scoops Old-Fashioned Vanilla Ice Cream | 6 |
| 4 | egg whites or $^1/_2$ cup (125 mL) liquid pasteurized egg whites (see Tip, below) | 4 |
| $^1/_4$ tsp | cream of tartar | 1 mL |
| $^3/_4$ cup | granulated sugar | 175 mL |

1. Place cookies on prepared baking sheet. Top each with one scoop ice cream. Freeze for 1 hour or until hard.

2. Meanwhile, in a bowl, beat egg whites until foamy. Add cream of tartar and beat until soft peaks form.

3. Gradually add sugar. Continue to beat until stiff glossy peaks form.

4. Remove the ice cream and cookies from the freezer. Using a spatula or spoon and working quickly, spread meringue completely over ice cream and cookies, making certain to cover all the ice cream right down to the cookie crust.

5. Bake in preheated oven until golden brown, about 6 minutes. Serve immediately.

**Tip:** $^1/_2$ cup (125 mL) liquid pasteurized egg whites is equivalent to 4 fresh egg whites. Egg whites are now available in cartons in the supermarket dairy section. They're great to have on hand for egg white omelets (no cholesterol) or to make angel food cake.

SERVES 6

# Orange Custard Ice Cream

**SERVES 8 TO 10**

**Tip:** If you adore orange, you can increase the amount of orange extract to 3 tbsp (45 mL).

**Serving suggestion:** For a fancy dinner party, slice one-third off the tops of 6 oranges. (You will need an additional orange for zesting.) Set tops aside. Squeeze juice out of bottoms, then scrape out any membranes. Scoop Orange Custard Ice Cream into shells. Top with lids. Freeze until firm.

*This tangy and creamy ice cream gets its flavor from the combination of whipping cream and buttermilk. One spoonful and you'll be transported back in time to the hot, hazy summer days of your childhood. Serve it plain or garnished with a sprig of fresh mint or a piece of orange-flavored chocolate.*

| 5 | egg yolks | 5 |
|---|---|---|
| 1 1/4 cups | granulated sugar | 300 mL |
| 2 cups | whipping (35%) cream | 500 mL |
| 2 cups | buttermilk | 500 mL |
| | Zest of 1 orange | |
| 1/2 cup | freshly squeezed orange juice | 125 mL |
| 2 tbsp | orange extract | 25 mL |

1. In a bowl, whisk egg yolks with sugar until thickened and pale yellow. Set aside.

2. In a medium saucepan over medium-low heat, bring cream and buttermilk to a simmer. Gradually whisk into the egg mixture.

3. Return entire mixture to the saucepan. Cook over low heat, stirring constantly, until the mixture is thick enough to coat the back of a wooden spoon. Be careful not to let it boil. Strain into a clean large bowl. Let cool to room temperature.

4. Stir in orange zest, orange juice and orange extract. Cover and refrigerate until completely cold or overnight.

5. Transfer to an ice cream maker and freeze according to manufacturer's instructions.

---

**VARIATIONS:** *Chocolate Orange Custard Ice Cream: Add 1/2 cup (125 mL) shaved orange-flavored chocolate in the last 5 minutes of freezing and let machine stir it in.*

*Orange Lime Custard Ice Cream: Reduce orange juice to 1/4 cup (50 mL) and add 1/4 cup (50 mL) freshly squeezed lime juice.*

# Orange Marmalade Ice Cream

**SERVES 8 TO 10**

**Tip:** This ice cream can be a little softer than egg-based ice creams, so don't worry if it's a little sloppy. If you prefer it harder, pop it in the freezer overnight.

*This ice cream is so easy to make that it's almost like cheating. It uses store-bought marmalade, requires no cooking and is soft, luscious and oh-so-delicious.*

| | | |
|---|---|---|
| 2 cups | orange marmalade | 500 mL |
| I tbsp | vanilla | 15 mL |
| I tbsp | orange extract | 15 mL |
| 2 cups | table (18%) cream | 500 mL |
| 2 cups | milk | 500 mL |

1. In a large bowl, stir together marmalade, vanilla and orange extract. Stir in cream and milk.

2. Cover and refrigerate until completely cold or overnight.

3. Transfer to an ice cream maker and freeze according to manufacturer's instructions.

> **VARIATION:** *Jam Ice Cream: Omit orange extract. Instead of the orange marmalade, substitute your favorite jam, such as raspberry, apricot or strawberry.*

# Peach Ice Cream

**SERVES 6 TO 8**

**Tip:** This is a good crisper cleaner, especially during the last days of summer, when you have an assortment of fruits in the refrigerator. Fruits such as peaches, plums, strawberries and raspberries are perfect for this. (Apples wouldn't work.) The juicier the peaches, the better.

*This ice cream is the perfect accompaniment to a home-baked peach pie. The recipe calls for fresh peaches, but if you crave it out of season, one can (14 oz/398 mL) peaches, drained, will do just fine.*

| | | |
|---|---|---|
| 4 | peaches, peeled and pitted | 4 |
| 2 tbsp | freshly squeezed lime juice | 25 mL |
| 6 | egg yolks | 6 |
| 2/3 cup | granulated sugar | 150 mL |
| 1 1/2 cups | table (18%) cream | 375 mL |
| 1 1/2 cups | milk | 375 mL |
| 1 tbsp | vanilla | 15 mL |

1. In a food processor or blender, purée peaches with lime juice until smooth. Push purée through a fine sieve to remove any tough pieces of skin. Set aside.

2. In a bowl, whisk egg yolks with sugar until thickened and pale yellow. Set aside.

3. In a medium saucepan over medium-low heat, bring cream and milk to a simmer. Gradually whisk into the egg mixture.

4. Return entire mixture to the saucepan. Cook over low heat, stirring constantly, until the mixture is thick enough to coat the back of a wooden spoon. Be careful not to let it boil. Strain into a clean large bowl. Let cool to room temperature.

5. Stir in peach purée and vanilla. Cover and refrigerate until completely cold or overnight.

6. Transfer to an ice cream maker and freeze according to manufacturer's instructions.

> **VARIATIONS:** *Cardamom Peach Ice Cream: Add 1 tsp (5 mL) ground cardamom to hot strained cream mixture.*
>
> *Blackberry Peach Ice Cream: Add 1 cup (250 mL) blackberries to food processor along with peaches and lime juice.*

# Peach Melba Ice Cream

*Peaches and raspberries, the foundation of this fabulous dessert — named after the Australian opera star Nellie Melba — are terrific swirled into an ice cream base.*

**SERVES 6 TO 8**

**Tip:** You may want to make this when fresh raspberries and peaches are not available. If so, substitute 1 can (14 oz/398 mL) sliced peaches, drained, and an additional ¼ cup (50 mL) raspberry jam mixed with the orange juice.

**Serving suggestion:** For a spectacular finish to a dinner party, serve this sparkler. In a food processor or blender, purée 1 cup (250 mL) chopped pitted peeled fresh peaches with 1 cup (250 mL) fresh raspberries. Divide purée among champagne glasses. Add 1 scoop of Peach Melba Ice Cream or store-bought raspberry sherbet. Top with sparkling wine and a sprig of fresh mint.

| | | |
|---|---|---|
| 3 | ripe peaches, peeled, pitted and chopped | 3 |
| 1 cup | Simple Syrup (see recipe, page 23) | 250 mL |
| 1 cup | whipping (35%) cream | 250 mL |
| 1 cup | milk | 250 mL |
| 1 cup | fresh raspberries | 250 mL |
| ¼ cup | raspberry jam | 50 mL |
| ¼ cup | orange juice | 50 mL |

1. In a food processor or blender, purée peaches with syrup until smooth. Transfer to a clean large bowl. Stir in cream and milk. Cover and refrigerate until completely cold or overnight.

2. Transfer to an ice cream maker and freeze according to manufacturer's instructions.

3. Meanwhile, in a food processor or blender, purée raspberries, jam and orange juice until smooth.

4. When the ice cream is almost frozen, pack half of it into a freezerproof container. Spoon in half of the raspberry mixture. Repeat layers once.

5. Gently swirl raspberry mixture into ice cream with a knife. Cover and freeze until firm.

# Peanut Butter Chocolate Ice Cream

**SERVES 8 TO 10**

**Tip:** This ice cream will be soft. For firmer ice cream, place in the freezer for at least 2 hours.

*For many people, this is the ultimate combination. We leave the decision of whether to use smooth or chunky peanut butter up to you. The better the chocolate, the better this tastes.*

| | | |
|---|---|---|
| 3 | eggs | 3 |
| 1 1/2 cups | granulated sugar | 375 mL |
| 8 oz | bittersweet chocolate, finely chopped | 250 g |
| 2 cups | half-and-half (10%) cream | 500 mL |
| 1 cup | whipping (35%) cream | 250 mL |
| 1 tsp | vanilla | 5 mL |
| 3/4 cup | peanut butter | 175 mL |

1. In a bowl, whisk eggs with sugar until thickened and pale yellow. Set aside.

2. In a medium saucepan, combine chocolate and half-and-half. Cook over low heat, stirring occasionally, until chocolate is melted. Gradually whisk into the egg mixture.

3. Return entire mixture to the saucepan. Cook over low heat, stirring constantly, until the mixture is thick enough to coat the back of a wooden spoon. Be careful not to let it boil. Strain into a clean large bowl. Let cool to room temperature.

4. Stir in whipping cream and vanilla. Cover and refrigerate until completely cold or overnight.

5. Stir cream mixture. Transfer 1 cup (250 mL) to a small bowl. Whisk in peanut butter until blended. Stir peanut butter mixture into remaining cream mixture.

6. Transfer to an ice cream maker and freeze according to manufacturer's instructions.

# Peppermint Chocolate Chip Ice Cream

**SERVES 6**

**Tip:** You can use crème de menthe to make this ice cream green and extra minty. Add only 1 tbsp (15 mL) crème de menthe to the strained cream mixture or the ice cream won't freeze properly.

**Serving suggestion:** To dress up this dessert, serve scoops in store-bought chocolate cups, available at grocery stores. Garnish with sprigs of fresh mint.

*This cool, refreshing ice cream is a hit with both kids and adults. Just ask five-year-old Charley, who gobbles it up whenever it's made. If you're a true fan of this classic combo, you might want to add some green food coloring to make sure it looks minty. This version is white and packs a refreshing punch.*

| | | |
|---|---|---|
| 2 | egg yolks | 2 |
| 3/4 cup | granulated sugar | 175 mL |
| 1 cup | whipping (35%) cream | 250 mL |
| 1 cup | table (18%) cream | 250 mL |
| 1 cup | milk | 250 mL |
| 2 tbsp | peppermint extract | 25 mL |
| 1/2 cup | finely chopped bittersweet chocolate | 125 mL |

1. In a bowl, whisk egg yolks with sugar until thickened and pale yellow. Set aside.

2. In a medium saucepan over medium-low heat, bring whipping cream, table cream and milk to a simmer. Gradually whisk into the egg mixture.

3. Return entire mixture to the saucepan. Cook over low heat, stirring constantly, until the mixture is thick enough to coat the back of a wooden spoon. Be careful not to let it boil. Strain into a clean large bowl. Let cool to room temperature.

4. Stir in peppermint extract. Cover and refrigerate until completely cold or overnight.

5. Transfer to an ice cream maker and freeze according to manufacturer's instructions. Add chocolate in the last 5 minutes of freezing and let machine stir it in.

**VARIATION:** *Double Mint Ice Cream: Substitute 1/2 cup (125 mL) chopped chocolate-covered after-dinner mint wafers for bittersweet chocolate.*

# Pistachio Ice Cream

**SERVES 6**

**Tip:** This ice cream will be soft. For firmer ice cream, place in the freezer for at least 2 hours.

*Use unsalted, preferably peeled, raw pistachios for this beautiful pale green ice cream. For a savory finish, dust the top of each serving with crushed salted pistachios. Though this ice cream is very green, if you want it neon, you can add a drop of green food coloring.*

| | | |
|---|---|---|
| 1 1/2 cups | shelled unsalted raw pistachios, divided | 375 mL |
| 1/2 cup | corn syrup | 125 mL |
| 1/2 cup | half-and-half (10%) cream | 125 mL |
| 1 cup | table (18%) cream | 250 mL |
| 1/4 cup | granulated sugar | 50 mL |
| 1 cup | whipping (35%) cream | 250 mL |
| 3/4 tsp | vanilla | 4 mL |
| 1/4 tsp | salt | 1 mL |
| 1/4 tsp | almond extract | 1 mL |

1. In a food processor or blender, purée 1 cup (250 mL) pistachios, corn syrup and half-and-half until smooth.

2. In a medium saucepan over medium-low heat, bring table cream to a simmer. Add sugar and stir until sugar is dissolved.

3. With the food processor running, gradually pour cream mixture into pistachio mixture. Purée until smooth.

4. Strain into a clean large bowl. Stir in whipping cream, vanilla, salt and almond extract. Cover and refrigerate until completely cold or overnight.

5. Stir cream mixture. Transfer to an ice cream maker and freeze according to manufacturer's instructions. Add remaining pistachios in the last 5 minutes of freezing.

> **VARIATION: *Turkish Delight Pistachio Ice Cream:*** Substitute 1 tbsp (15 mL) rose water for the almond extract. Top each serving with a sprinkle of chopped Turkish delight candies.

# Pucker-Up Ice Cream

**SERVES 8**

**Tip:** Make sure to add the lemon and lime juice when the mixture is completely cold or the acid could curdle the cream mixture.

**Serving suggestion:** For a fabulous end to a dinner party, serve a scoop of Pucker-Up Ice Cream with a slice of lemon pound cake and a few fresh raspberries.

*There's nothing more refreshing than a tall, cool glass of lemonade in the summertime, which is why we expanded on a lemon float to make this ice cream. The creaminess combined with tart, juicy lemons really makes your taste buds tingle.*

| 4 | eggs yolks | 4 |
|---|---|---|
| 1¼ cups | granulated sugar | 300 mL |
| 2 cups | table (18%) cream | 500 mL |
| 2 cups | milk | 500 mL |
| | Zest of 2 lemons | |
| ½ cup | freshly squeezed lemon juice | 125 mL |
| | Zest of 1 lime | |
| ¼ cup | freshly squeezed lime juice | 50 mL |

1. In a bowl, whisk egg yolks with sugar until thickened and pale yellow. Set aside.

2. In a medium saucepan over medium-low heat, bring cream and milk to a simmer. Gradually whisk into the egg mixture.

3. Return entire mixture to the saucepan. Cook over low heat, stirring constantly, until mixture is thick enough to coat the back of a wooden spoon. Be careful not to let it boil. Strain into a clean large bowl. Let cool to room temperature. Cover and refrigerate until completely cold or overnight.

4. Stir in lemon zest and juice and lime zest and juice (see Tip, left). Transfer to an ice cream maker and freeze according to manufacturer's instructions.

**VARIATIONS: Grapefruit Pucker-Up Ice Cream:** *Substitute zest of 1 grapefruit and ¾ cup (175 mL) grapefruit juice for the lemon and lime zest and juice.*

**Lime Pucker-Up Ice Cream:** *Omit lemon zest and juice and increase lime zest to 3 limes and juice to ¾ cup (175 mL).*

# Pumpkin Ice Cream

**SERVES 8**

*If you can't wait until Thanksgiving for the taste of pumpkin pie, try making this ice cream instead. Don't bother using fresh pumpkin — the canned variety is silky smooth and the key to this recipe's success.*

**Tip:** Make sure you buy 100% pumpkin purée, not a blend of pumpkin and other squashes.

**Serving suggestion:** For a frozen pumpkin pie, spoon softened Pumpkin Ice Cream into a 9-inch (23 cm) store-bought graham cracker crust. Freeze until firm. To serve, top with whipped cream rosettes and chocolate shavings.

| | | |
|---|---|---|
| 4 | egg yolks | 4 |
| ¾ cup | granulated sugar | 175 mL |
| 2 cups | whipping (35%) cream | 500 mL |
| 2 cups | milk | 500 mL |
| I cup | unsweetened pumpkin purée (not pie filling) | 250 mL |
| I tsp | ground cinnamon | 5 mL |
| I tsp | ground nutmeg | 5 mL |
| I tsp | ground ginger | 5 mL |
| I tsp | vanilla | 5 mL |

**1.** In a bowl, whisk egg yolks with sugar until thickened and pale yellow. Set aside.

**2.** In a medium saucepan over medium-low heat, bring cream and milk to a simmer. Gradually whisk into the egg mixture.

**3.** Return entire mixture to the saucepan. Cook over low heat, stirring constantly, until the mixture is thick enough to coat the back of a wooden spoon. Be careful not to let it boil. Strain into a clean large bowl. Let cool to room temperature.

**4.** Whisk in pumpkin purée, in two additions, until smooth. Stir in cinnamon, nutmeg, ginger and vanilla. Cover and refrigerate until completely cold or overnight.

**5.** Stir cream mixture. Transfer to an ice cream maker and freeze according to manufacturer's instructions.

# Rice Pudding Ice Cream

**SERVES 4 TO 6**

**Tips:** This ice cream will be soft. For firmer ice cream, place in the freezer for at least 2 hours.

You'll need about ¹/₂ cup (125 mL) raw rice to make 1 cup (250 mL) cooked.

*We adore rice pudding and decided to turn this comfort food into ice cream. But instead of long-grain rice, we used the short-grain Arborio we rely on for risotto. Sometimes we add 1 cup (250 mL) golden raisins to the mix. Often we add 1 tbsp (15 mL) lemon or orange zest. This recipe is rather exotic, with its licorice-anise taste. You can substitute cinnamon in place of the aniseed for a more traditional flavor. It's a great dessert to complement an Indian dinner — especially if you replace the aniseed with cardamom.*

| | | |
|---|---|---|
| 1 cup | cooked Arborio or other short-grain rice (see Tips, left) | 250 mL |
| 1 cup | milk | 250 mL |
| 1 cup | table (18%) cream | 250 mL |
| ³⁄₄ cup | granulated sugar | 175 mL |
| 2 | eggs | 2 |
| ¹/₂ cup | whipping (35%) cream | 125 mL |
| 1 tsp | ground aniseed | 5 mL |
| ¹/₄ tsp | vanilla | 1 mL |

1. In a medium saucepan over medium heat, bring rice, milk, table cream and sugar to a simmer. Cook, stirring occasionally, until sugar is dissolved. Reduce heat to low. Simmer, stirring occasionally, for 30 minutes or until thick and creamy. Stir constantly in the last 5 minutes to prevent sticking. Be careful not to let it boil. Let cool to room temperature.

2. In a large bowl, whisk eggs until pale yellow. Gradually whisk in rice mixture.

3. Stir in whipping cream, aniseed and vanilla. Cover and refrigerate until completely cold or overnight.

4. Stir cream mixture. Transfer to an ice cream maker and freeze according to manufacturer's instructions.

# Instant Rice Pudding Ice Cream

*Rice pudding straight from the can makes an easy, velvety, delicious ice cream. You can add chopped candied fruit for a Christmassy version.*

**SERVES 6**

| | | |
|---|---|---|
| 2 | cans (each 15 oz/425 mL) rice pudding | 2 |
| 1 cup | Simple Syrup (see recipe, page 23) | 250 mL |
| 1/2 tsp | vanilla | 2 mL |
| | Zest of 1 lemon | |

1. In a bowl, stir together rice pudding, syrup, vanilla and lemon zest.

2. Transfer to an ice cream maker and freeze according to manufacturer's instructions.

---

**VARIATION: *Cinnamon-Spiced Instant Rice Pudding Ice Cream:*** *Add 1 tsp (5 mL) cinnamon and 1/4 tsp (1 mL) ground nutmeg to rice pudding mixture before freezing.*

# Orange Shredded Wheat Crisps

*For a crunchy topping to almost any ice cream or frozen yogurt, make these orange crisps one day ahead and store them in an airtight container.*

**PREHEAT OVEN TO 350°F (180°C)**
**RIMMED BAKING SHEET, GREASED**

| | | |
|---|---|---|
| 2 | large shredded wheat cereal biscuits | 2 |
| 1 tbsp | unsalted butter, melted | 15 mL |
| 2 tsp | packed brown sugar | 10 mL |
| $1/2$ tsp | orange zest | 2 mL |

1. Crumble biscuits into a bowl. Toss with butter, brown sugar and orange zest. Place on prepared baking sheet.

2. Bake in preheated oven until golden, about 10 minutes. Let cool to room temperature.

3. Serve as a topping for ice cream or frozen yogurt or mix into your favorite flavor in the last 5 minutes of freezing and let machine stir it in.

**SERVES 6**

# Roasted Garlic Ice Cream

**SERVES 4 TO 6**

**Tip:** This ice cream will be soft. For firmer ice cream, place in the freezer for at least 2 hours.

*Roasting garlic mellows its flavor and gives it a bit of a nuttiness. But make no mistake: this ice cream is for garlic lovers only. Some recipes call for five heads of garlic, which, to us, sounds like a bit of overkill.*

**PREHEAT OVEN TO 350°F (180°C)**

| | | |
|---|---|---|
| 2 | heads garlic | 2 |
| 2 tsp | olive oil | 10 mL |
| 3 | egg yolks | 3 |
| 1/4 cup | granulated sugar | 50 mL |
| 1 cup | table (18%) cream | 250 mL |
| 1/2 cup | 2% milk (see Tips, page 30) | 125 mL |
| 1 cup | whipping (35%) cream | 250 mL |
| 1/8 tsp | salt | 0.5 mL |

1. Cut 1/4 inch (0.5 cm) off tops of garlic heads. Place each head on a large square of foil. Drizzle with oil. Pull up foil around garlic and seal to make two packages. Roast in preheated oven for 30 minutes.

2. Open foil to expose garlic. Return to oven and roast for another 30 minutes or until soft and browned. Remove from oven. When cool enough to handle, squeeze garlic out into bowl. Set aside.

3. In a separate bowl, whisk egg yolks with sugar until thickened and pale yellow. Set aside.

**4.** In a medium saucepan over medium-low heat, bring table cream, milk and half of the roasted garlic to a simmer. Reduce heat to low. Simmer, stirring often, for 15 minutes or until thickened. Gradually whisk into the egg mixture.

**5.** Return entire mixture to the saucepan. Cook over low heat, stirring constantly, until the mixture is thick enough to coat the back of a wooden spoon. Be careful not to let it boil. Strain into a clean large bowl. Let cool to room temperature.

**6.** Stir in whipping cream and salt. Cover and refrigerate until completely cold or overnight.

**7.** Stir the cream mixture. Transfer to an ice cream maker and freeze according to manufacturer's instructions. Add remaining roasted garlic in the last 5 minutes of freezing and let machine stir it in.

# Rosemary Ice Cream

## SERVES 6 TO 8

**Tip:** For more intense flavor, simmer the rosemary-cream mixture for 30 minutes. For just a hint of rosemary flavor, simmer the mixture for 5 minutes.

**Serving suggestions:** Line a muffin tin with paper muffin cups. Place one scoop of Rosemary Ice Cream into each cup. Freeze until firm. When ready to serve, lift out the cups and tear off the paper liners for tidy, one-serving portions. Or place two scoops in a bowl and garnish with a small sprig of fresh rosemary and a sugar, shortbread or lavender cookie.

*Want an elegant ice cream to serve at your next dinner party? Try this simple yet sophisticated recipe for rosemary-infused ice cream. Its sweet, aromatic flavor is sure to be a delicious topic of conversation at any table.*

| 3 | egg yolks | 3 |
|---|---|---|
| 1/2 cup | granulated sugar | 125 mL |
| 1 tbsp | packed brown sugar | 15 mL |
| 2 cups | table (18%) cream | 500 mL |
| 2 cups | milk | 500 mL |
| 4 | sprigs fresh rosemary (see Tip, left and page 125) | 4 |

1. In a bowl, whisk egg yolks with granulated and brown sugars until thickened and pale yellow. Set aside.

2. In a medium saucepan over medium-low heat, bring cream, milk and rosemary to a simmer. Simmer, stirring occasionally, for 15 minutes. Discard rosemary. Gradually whisk hot cream mixture into the egg mixture.

3. Return entire mixture to the saucepan. Cook over low heat, stirring constantly, until the mixture is thick enough to coat the back of a wooden spoon. Be careful not to let it boil. Strain into a clean large bowl. Let cool to room temperature. Cover and refrigerate until completely cold or overnight.

4. Stir cream mixture. Transfer to an ice cream maker and freeze according to manufacturer's instructions.

> **VARIATION:** *Lavender Ice Cream: Substitute 4 sprigs fresh lavender flowers for the rosemary.*

Strawberries and Cream Ice Cream (page 98)
*Overleaf:* Tomato Basil Ice (page 147)
and Blueberry Ginger Ice (page 125)

# Rum Raisin Ice Cream

**SERVES 6 TO 8**

*Use plump golden raisins and premium rum. Serve on its own or as a complement to bananas sautéed with brown sugar and butter.*

| | | |
|---|---|---|
| 1½ cups | golden raisins | 375 mL |
| ⅓ cup | orange juice | 75 mL |
| 2 | eggs | 2 |
| ¾ cup | packed light brown sugar | 175 mL |
| 1 cup | half-and-half (10%) cream | 250 mL |
| 1 cup | whipping (35%) cream | 250 mL |
| ¼ cup | dark rum | 50 mL |

1. In a bowl, toss raisins with orange juice. Let stand for 1 hour.

2. Meanwhile, in a separate bowl, whisk eggs with sugar until thickened and pale yellow. Set aside.

3. In a medium saucepan over medium-low heat, bring half-and-half and whipping cream to a simmer. Gradually whisk into the egg mixture.

4. Return entire mixture to the saucepan. Cook over low heat, stirring constantly, until the mixture is thick enough to coat the back of a wooden spoon. Be careful not to let it boil. Strain into a clean large bowl. Let cool to room temperature.

5. Stir in raisin mixture and rum. Cover and refrigerate until completely cold or overnight.

6. Stir cream mixture. Transfer to an ice cream maker and freeze according to manufacturer's instructions.

Chocolate Chip Coffee Gelato (page 107)

# Strawberries and Cream Ice Cream

*This intensely fruity ice cream is best made with the sweetest and juiciest of fresh berries. It's terrific on its own or as a topping for waffles and crêpes.*

**Tip:** If possible, taste the berries before buying them to ensure the best flavor.

**Serving suggestion:** For a quick Strawberry Sauce, in a food processor or blender, purée 1 cup (250 mL) additional strawberries with 2 tbsp (25 mL) orange juice, Cointreau or white vermouth. Pour over ice cream.

| | | |
|---|---|---|
| 2 cups | whipping (35%) cream | 500 mL |
| 1/2 cup | granulated sugar | 125 mL |
| 4 cups | fresh strawberries, hulled | 1 L |
| 1/4 cup | freshly squeezed orange juice | 50 mL |
| 1 tbsp | orange zest | 15 mL |

1. In a medium saucepan over medium-low heat, bring cream to a simmer. Stir in sugar. Cook, stirring, until sugar is dissolved. Let cool to room temperature.

2. In a food processor or blender, purée strawberries with orange juice until smooth. Stir into cream mixture along with orange zest. Cover and refrigerate until completely cold or overnight.

3. Transfer to an ice cream maker and freeze according to manufacturer's instructions.

# Strawberry-Rhubarb Ice Cream

**SERVES 8**

**Tip:** You can use either fresh or frozen rhubarb.

*The combination of these two fruits is a classic, so much so that it's worth the extra effort to prepare and cook the rhubarb.*

| 2 cups | chopped rhubarb, about ½-inch (1 cm) pieces | 500 mL |
| ½ cup | water | 125 mL |
| 2 | eggs | 2 |
| ⅔ cup | granulated sugar | 150 mL |
| 1 cup | milk | 250 mL |
| 1 cup | whipping (35%) cream | 250 mL |
| 2 cups | chopped ripe strawberries | 500 mL |

1. In a medium saucepan over medium heat, bring rhubarb and water to a simmer. Cook, stirring occasionally, for 15 minutes or until rhubarb is soft and mixture resembles thick applesauce. Using the back of a wooden spoon, push through a fine sieve. Set aside.

2. In a bowl, whisk eggs with sugar until thickened and pale yellow. Set aside.

3. In a separate medium saucepan over medium-low heat, bring milk and cream to a simmer. Gradually whisk into the egg mixture.

4. Return entire mixture to the saucepan. Cook over low heat, stirring constantly, until the mixture is thick enough to coat the back of a wooden spoon. Be careful not to let it boil. Strain into a clean large bowl. Let cool to room temperature.

5. Stir in rhubarb mixture and strawberries. Cover and refrigerate until completely cold or overnight.

6. Stir cream mixture. Transfer to an ice cream maker and freeze according to manufacturer's instructions.

> **VARIATION:** *Ginger Strawberry-Rhubarb Ice Cream: Add 2 tbsp (25 mL) chopped crystallized ginger to the strained cream mixture.*

# Tiramisu Ice Cream

*This traditional Italian layered dessert is now on many ice cream-shop menus. Because it is meant to be shown off as well as enjoyed, we layer ours in a pretty glass bowl and return it to the freezer until firm. You can also spoon it into parfait glasses and freeze until you're ready to serve.*

| | | |
|---|---|---|
| 1 cup | granulated sugar, divided | 250 mL |
| 1 cup | water | 250 mL |
| 1 cup | mascarpone cheese | 250 mL |
| 1 cup | cream cheese, softened | 250 mL |
| 1 1/2 tsp | vanilla | 7 mL |
| 3 tbsp | boiling water | 45 mL |
| 1 tbsp | instant coffee granules | 15 mL |
| 3 tbsp | coffee-flavored liqueur | 45 mL |
| 3 oz | ladyfingers (about 6) | 90 g |
| 1/4 cup | unsweetened cocoa powder | 50 mL |
| 1/4 cup | bittersweet chocolate shavings | 50 mL |

1. Combine 3/4 cup (175 mL) sugar and 1 cup (250 mL) water in a medium saucepan. Cook over medium-low heat, stirring, until sugar is dissolved. Let cool to room temperature, about 15 minutes.

2. In a medium bowl, beat mascarpone cheese with a wooden spoon until soft. Stir in cream cheese. Whisk in sugar syrup, 2 tbsp (25 mL) at a time, until well blended. Stir in vanilla. Cover and refrigerate until completely cold or overnight.

3. Meanwhile, in a bowl, stir together boiling water, remaining sugar and instant coffee. Stir in liqueur. Let cool to room temperature, about 15 minutes.

4. Stir cheese mixture. Transfer to an ice cream maker and freeze according to manufacturer's instructions.

5. Crumble ladyfingers into small pieces. Toss with coffee mixture. Set aside.

6. Spoon one-third of the ice cream into a freezerproof container, glass serving bowl or parfait glasses. Layer half of the biscuit mixture over top. Repeat layers once. Top with remaining ice cream. Freeze for 2 to 3 hours or until firm.

7. To serve, dust with cocoa and sprinkle with chocolate shavings.

# Tropical Ice Cream

**SERVES 8**

*Take your taste buds on a trip to the tropics with this coconut ice cream flavored with grated ginger and fresh lime juice. You won't believe this tangy dessert is made from pure unsweetened coconut milk — and the best part is that there is no cooking required.*

**Tip:** Because there is no cooking in this recipe, you can go straight to the ice cream maker if you use chilled coconut milk and cream.

**Serving suggestions:** Slice fresh kiwifruit, limes, mangoes and papaya to garnish two scoops of ice cream. Top with a piece of crystallized ginger.

| 2 | cans (each 14 oz/398 mL) unsweetened coconut milk | 2 |
|---|---|---|
| 1 cup | granulated sugar | 250 mL |
| 1 cup | half-and-half (10%) cream | 250 mL |
| | Zest of 1 lime | |
| 1/3 cup | freshly squeezed lime juice | 75 mL |
| 1/3 cup | grated gingerroot | 75 mL |

1. In a bowl, whisk together coconut milk, sugar, half-and-half, lime zest and juice, and ginger until sugar is dissolved and mixture is smooth.

2. Cover and refrigerate until completely cold or overnight.

3. Stir cream mixture. Transfer to an ice cream maker and freeze according to manufacturer's instructions.

# Tutti-Frutti Ice Cream

**SERVES 6 TO 8**

**Tip:** This ice cream will be soft. For firmer ice cream, place in the freezer for at least 2 hours.

*Any or all of the candied fruits of your choosing can be added to this rich vanilla base. For a truly Christmassy dessert, serve with a slice of your favorite fruitcake. Or toss a few slices of fruitcake, crumbled, into the ice cream in the last 5 minutes of freezing.*

| | | |
|---|---|---|
| 3 | egg yolks | 3 |
| 1/3 cup | superfine sugar | 75 mL |
| 1 | vanilla bean | 1 |
| 1 1/2 cups | 2% milk (see Tips, page 30) | 375 mL |
| 1 1/2 cups | whipping (35%) cream | 375 mL |
| 1 1/4 cups | chopped mixed candied fruit (such as green and red cherries, pineapple, mango, papaya, lime peel and/or orange peel) | 300 mL |

1. In a bowl, whisk egg yolks with sugar until thickened and pale yellow. Set aside.

2. Slit vanilla bean lengthwise and scrape seeds into a medium saucepan. Add vanilla pod, milk and cream. Place the saucepan over medium-low heat and bring just to a simmer. Remove from heat. Let stand for 15 minutes, allowing the flavor of the vanilla to infuse.

3. Discard pod. Bring to a simmer over medium-low heat and simmer for 5 minutes. Gradually whisk into the egg mixture.

4. Return entire mixture to the saucepan. Cook over low heat, stirring constantly, until the mixture is thick enough to coat the back of a wooden spoon. Be careful not to let it boil. Strain into a clean large bowl. Let cool to room temperature. Cover and refrigerate until completely cold or overnight.

5. Stir cream mixture. Transfer to an ice cream maker and freeze according to manufacturer's instructions. Add candied fruit in the last 5 minutes of freezing and let machine stir it in.

# White Chocolate Ice Cream

**SERVES 6 TO 8**

**Serving suggestions:**
Serve with
fresh raspberries,
blueberries or
strawberries.

*White chocolate seems like an extravagant ingredient in ice cream, but everyone enjoys a little indulgence now and then. This is a simple and elegant ice cream that is bound to impress at the end of a formal dinner. Rest assured, however, that it's as binge-worthy as many others. Because of its rich flavor, this dessert requires no eggs to thicken it or to add texture.*

| 2 cups | whipping (35%) cream | 500 mL |
| 2 cups | milk | 500 mL |
| 1/3 cup | granulated sugar | 75 mL |
| 8 oz | white chocolate, coarsely chopped | 250 g |
| 2 tsp | vanilla | 10 mL |

1. In a medium saucepan over medium-low heat, bring cream, milk and sugar to a simmer.

2. Place white chocolate in a bowl. Pour cream mixture over top and let stand for 5 minutes. Whisk until smooth. Whisk in vanilla.

3. Cover and refrigerate until completely cold or overnight.

4. Stir cream mixture. Transfer to an ice cream maker and freeze according to manufacturer's instructions.

> **VARIATIONS: *White Chocolate Cranberry Pistachio Ice Cream:*** *Add 1/4 cup (50 mL) dried cranberries and 1/4 cup (50 mL) chopped raw unsalted pistachios in the last 5 minutes of freezing and let machine stir them in.*
>
> ***White Chocolate Ginger Ice Cream:*** *Add 1/4 cup (50 mL) finely chopped crystallized ginger in the last 5 minutes of freezing and let machine stir it in.*

# GELATOS

# Bubble Gelato

SERVES 6

*Inspired by both a childhood love of tapioca pudding and a fascination with the bubble tea that's so popular in Asian tea shops, we created an easy milk-based gelato that all ages seem to adore. You can buy instant tapioca in any supermarket. Anyone on a gluten-free diet can enjoy this treat.*

| | | |
|---|---|---|
| 3 cups | milk | 750 mL |
| 1/2 cup | granulated sugar | 125 mL |
| 3 tbsp | tapioca granules | 45 mL |
| I | egg | I |
| I tbsp | vanilla | 15 mL |
| | Zest of I lemon | |

1. In a medium saucepan without the heat on, whisk together milk, sugar, tapioca and egg. Let stand for 3 minutes. Place saucepan over medium heat and bring to a boil, stirring constantly. Transfer to a bowl (do not strain).

2. Stir in vanilla and lemon zest. Let cool to room temperature. Cover and refrigerate until completely cold or overnight.

3. Stir milk mixture. Transfer to an ice cream maker and freeze according to manufacturer's instructions.

# Chocolate Chip Coffee Gelato

**SERVES 4**

**Serving suggestion:**
Sprinkle 2 tsp
(10 mL) sliced
almonds, chopped
hazelnuts or
chopped pecans
over each serving.

*This gelato pleases both the coffee lover and the chocoholic. If you're really addicted to coffee, double the coffee granules for a real kick.*

| | | |
|---|---|---|
| 2 cups | milk, divided | 500 mL |
| 2 tbsp | cornstarch | 25 mL |
| 1/3 cup | granulated sugar | 75 mL |
| 3 tbsp | unsweetened cocoa powder | 45 mL |
| 1 1/2 tbsp | instant coffee granules | 22 mL |
| 1 tbsp | vanilla | 15 mL |
| 2 oz | bittersweet chocolate, finely chopped, divided | 60 g |

1. In a small bowl, whisk 1/2 cup (125 mL) milk with cornstarch until smooth. Set aside.

2. In a medium saucepan over medium heat, whisk together remaining milk, sugar and cocoa powder. Bring to a simmer, stirring often. Whisk in coffee granules. Whisk the cornstarch mixture to recombine. Gradually whisk into sugar mixture. Return to a boil, stirring often. Strain into a clean large bowl. Let cool to room temperature.

3. Stir in vanilla and half of the chocolate. Cover and refrigerate until completely cold or overnight.

4. Stir milk mixture. Transfer to an ice cream maker and freeze according to manufacturer's instructions. Add remaining chocolate during last 5 minutes of freezing and let machine stir it in.

# Cinnamon Gelato

**SERVES 6**

*We love to serve this gelato in February, dusted with powdered cinnamon and sprinkled with red cinnamon hearts. Use fresh cinnamon sticks to make the base.*

| 4 | egg yolks | 4 |
|---|---|---|
| I cup | granulated sugar | 250 mL |
| 3 cups | milk | 750 mL |
| 3 | cinnamon sticks, broken into pieces | 3 |
| I | bay leaf | I |

1. In a bowl, whisk egg yolks with sugar until thickened and pale yellow. Set aside.

2. In a medium saucepan over medium heat, bring milk, cinnamon sticks and bay leaf to a simmer. Cook for 10 minutes. Remove from heat and let stand for 15 minutes. Strain into a clean large bowl, discarding cinnamon sticks and bay leaf. Gradually whisk into the egg mixture.

3. Return entire mixture to the saucepan. Cook over low heat, stirring constantly, until the mixture is thick enough to coat the back of a wooden spoon. Be careful not to let it boil. Let cool to room temperature. Cover and refrigerate until completely cold or overnight.

4. Transfer to an ice cream maker and freeze according to manufacturer's instructions.

> **VARIATION:** *Chocolate Peanut Butter Cinnamon Gelato:*
> *Chop 6 chocolate peanut butter cups into small pieces and add in the last 5 minutes of freezing. Allow chocolate peanut butter cups to mix in slightly.*

# Grape Gelato

*Although this gelato doesn't turn the color of a fine Merlot, its pinkish hue has eye appeal. Pour a little cassis syrup over each serving for extra flavor.*

| 4 | egg yolks | 4 |
| 3/4 cup | granulated sugar, divided | 175 mL |
| 3 cups | milk | 750 mL |
| 2 lbs | seedless red grapes | 1 kg |
| 1 cup | white grape juice | 250 mL |

1. In a bowl, whisk egg yolks with 6 tbsp (90 mL) sugar until thickened and pale yellow. Set aside

2. In a medium saucepan over medium-low heat, heat milk until bubbles appear around the edge. Gradually whisk into egg mixture, stirring constantly.

3. Return entire mixture to the saucepan. Cook over low heat, stirring constantly, until the mixture is thick enough to coat the back of a wooden spoon. Be careful not to let it boil. Strain into a clean large bowl. Let cool to room temperature. Cover and refrigerate until completely cold or overnight.

4. Meanwhile, in a separate saucepan over medium-low heat, cook grapes, juice and remaining sugar, stirring occasionally, until mixture is thickened. Let cool.

5. In a food processor or blender, purée grape mixture with chilled custard until smooth.

6. Transfer to an ice cream maker and freeze according to manufacturer's instructions.

# Kiwi Gelato

**SERVES 4 TO 6**

*Though often used to make ices, kiwifruit also makes a novel but yummy ice cream. Whether you use green kiwifruits or the new gold variety, it's essential that they be very ripe and soft when squeezed.*

| | | |
|---|---|---|
| 5 | large kiwifruits, peeled and sliced | 5 |
| ½ cup | Simple Syrup (see recipe, page 23) | 125 mL |
| ½ cup | milk | 125 mL |
| ¼ cup | whipping (35%) cream | 50 mL |
| ½ tsp | vanilla | 2 mL |

1. In a food processor or blender, purée kiwifruits with syrup until smooth.

2. Add milk, cream and vanilla. Pulse until well blended. Pour into a clean large bowl (do not strain). Cover and refrigerate until completely cold.

3. Stir milk mixture. Transfer to an ice cream maker and freeze according to manufacturer's instructions.

# Mascarpone Vanilla Gelato with Pine Nuts

**SERVES 4 TO 6**

*A fragrant infusion made with a vanilla bean gives this recipe real panache. Let the nuts cool to room temperature before adding them to the semifrozen mixture.*

**Tip:** Toast pine nuts just until golden in a toaster oven or dry skillet over medium-high heat. Whichever method you choose, keep stirring the nuts, as they can burn quickly. Let cool to room temperature before adding them to the machine.

| | | |
|---|---|---|
| 1 cup | milk | 250 mL |
| 1 cup | whipping (35%) cream | 250 mL |
| 1/2 cup | granulated sugar | 125 mL |
| 1 | vanilla bean | 1 |
| 1 cup | mascarpone cheese | 250 mL |
| 1/3 cup | toasted pine nuts (see Tip, left) | 75 mL |
| 1 tbsp | lemon zest | 15 mL |

1. In a medium saucepan over medium heat, combine milk, cream and sugar. Simmer, stirring, until sugar is dissolved and bubbles form around the edge of the saucepan. Remove from heat.

2. Slit vanilla bean lengthwise. Scrape seeds into the milk mixture. Add vanilla pod. Let stand for 30 minutes. Strain into a clean large bowl, discarding vanilla pod. Cover and refrigerate until completely cold or overnight.

3. Stir in mascarpone cheese, pine nuts and lemon zest. Transfer to an ice cream maker and freeze according to manufacturer's instructions.

# Passion Fruit Gelato

**SERVES 4 TO 6**

**Serving suggestion:**
Serve a scoop of
Passion Fruit Gelato
with a fresh fruit
salad or puréed
passion fruit.

*Fresh fruit is always a good way to add flavor to frozen desserts, so take advantage of what's in season. This gelato features passion fruit to give it a sweet-tart taste and an orangish hue.*

| | | |
|---|---|---|
| 4 | egg yolks | 4 |
| 1/2 cup | granulated sugar | 125 mL |
| 2 cups | milk | 500 mL |
| 4 | passion fruits | 4 |
| 1 tsp | vanilla | 5 mL |

1. In a bowl, whisk egg yolks with sugar until thickened and pale yellow. Set aside.

2. In a medium saucepan over medium-low heat, bring milk to a simmer, stirring occasionally. Gradually whisk into egg mixture.

3. Return entire mixture to the saucepan. Cook over low heat, stirring often, until the mixture is thick enough to coat the back of a wooden spoon. Be careful not to let it boil. Strain into a clean large bowl. Let cool to room temperature. Cover and refrigerate until completely cold or overnight.

4. Remove pulp and seeds from passion fruits to make about 1 cup (250 mL). Stir into milk mixture along with vanilla.

5. Transfer to an ice cream maker and freeze according to manufacturer's instructions.

> **VARIATION:** *Raspberry-Passion Fruit Gelato: Add 1/4 cup (50 mL) puréed raspberries along with passion fruit pulp and seeds before freezing.*

# Pear Ginger Ricotta Gelato

**SERVES 8 TO 10**

**Tip:** Do not add pears to the hot mixture — the heat will turn the pears to mush.

*Ricotta cheese is a great way to add creaminess to gelato. Here, it's partnered with pears and crystallized ginger to make an elegant frozen dessert. We found that canned pears packed in unsweetened juice added more flavor than fresh ones. You can always serve a scoop of this gelato with a poached pear to heighten the flavor.*

| | | |
|---|---|---|
| 3 cups | milk | 750 mL |
| 2 cups | ricotta cheese | 500 mL |
| 1/2 cup | granulated sugar | 125 mL |
| 1/4 cup | crystallized ginger, chopped | 50 mL |
| 1/4 tsp | vanilla | 1 mL |
| 1 | cinnamon stick | 1 |
| 1 | can (14 oz/398 mL) pear halves in unsweetened juice | 1 |

1. In a medium saucepan over medium heat, whisk together milk, ricotta cheese, sugar, ginger, vanilla and cinnamon stick. Bring just to a boil. Strain into a clean large bowl, discarding cinnamon stick. Let cool to room temperature.

2. Drain pears, reserving 3 tbsp (45 mL) juice. Chop pears. Stir pears into milk mixture along with reserved juice (see Tip, left). Cover and refrigerate until completely cold or overnight.

3. Stir milk mixture. Transfer to an ice cream maker and freeze according to manufacturer's instructions.

> **VARIATIONS:** *Peach Ginger Ricotta Gelato: Substitute 1 can (14 oz/398 mL) peach halves and 3 tbsp (45 mL) peach juice from can for the pears and pear juice.*
>
> *Lemon Ginger Ricotta Gelato: Omit pears and juice. Add zest of 1 lemon and 3 tbsp (45 mL) freshly squeezed lemon juice.*

# Persimmon Gelato

*Pumpkin pie gets a lift when served with this gelato made from fresh persimmons, an exotic fall fruit.*

**SERVES 4 TO 6**

| | | |
|---|---|---|
| 3 | fresh persimmons, peeled and pitted | 3 |
| I cup | Simple Syrup (see recipe, page 23) | 250 mL |
| I cup | whipping (35%) cream | 250 mL |
| I tsp | orange zest | 5 mL |

1. In a food processor or blender, purée persimmons with syrup until smooth. Transfer to a clean bowl.

2. In a separate bowl, whip cream. Fold into persimmon mixture. Stir in orange zest. Cover and refrigerate until completely cold or overnight.

3. Transfer to an ice cream maker and freeze according to manufacturer's instructions.

# Pineapple Mint Gelato

## SERVES 6 TO 8

**Tip:** Do not add chopped mint until the end, because it has a tendency to turn brown.

**Serving suggestion:** Place two scoops of Pineapple Mint Gelato in a cup along with freshly sliced pineapple and a sprinkle of sweetened flaked coconut.

*Pineapple is a fruit that most of us forget to use in ice creams, but it adds a zingy flavor to this gelato. Mint is a great garnish for this refreshing treat because it brings out the flavor of the pineapple.*

| | | |
|---|---|---|
| I | small ripe pineapple | I |
| 4 | egg yolks | 4 |
| ½ cup | granulated sugar | 125 mL |
| 2 cups | milk | 500 mL |
| I tsp | vanilla | 5 mL |
| 2 tbsp | chopped fresh mint | 25 mL |
| | (see Tip, left and page 125) | |

1. Peel and core pineapple and cut into chunks to make 2 cups (500 mL). In a food processor or blender, purée until smooth. Set aside.

2. In a bowl, whisk egg yolks with sugar until thickened and pale yellow. Set aside.

3. In a medium saucepan over medium-low heat, bring milk to a simmer, stirring occasionally. Gradually whisk into the egg mixture.

4. Return entire mixture to the saucepan. Cook over low heat, stirring often, until the mixture is thick enough to coat the back of a wooden spoon. Be careful not to let it boil. Strain into a clean large bowl. Let cool to room temperature. Cover and refrigerate until completely cold or overnight.

5. Stir in vanilla and pineapple purée. Transfer to an ice cream maker and freeze according to manufacturer's instructions. Just before serving, sprinkle with mint.

> **VARIATION:** *Tropical Gelato: Add 1 banana, mashed, to the custard mixture.*
>
> *Pineapple Orange Gelato: Omit mint. Stir in grated zest and juice of 1 orange along with the pineapple.*

# Strawberry Gelato

**SERVES 6 TO 8**

*Gelato is popular not only for its intense flavor and color but also because it's lighter than traditional ice cream. This one calls for milk but no cream.*

| | | |
|---|---|---|
| 4 | egg yolks | 4 |
| 1 cup | granulated sugar | 250 mL |
| 2 cups | milk | 500 mL |
| 2 cups | puréed strawberries, about 3 cups (750 mL) whole strawberries | 500 mL |
| 1/2 tsp | vanilla | 2 mL |

1. In a bowl, whisk egg yolks with sugar until thickened and pale yellow. Set aside.

2. In a medium saucepan over medium heat, bring milk to a simmer, stirring occasionally. Gradually whisk into the egg mixture.

3. Return entire mixture to the saucepan. Cook over low heat, stirring often, until the mixture is thick enough to coat the back of a wooden spoon. Be careful not to let it boil. Strain into a clean large bowl. Let cool to room temperature.

4. Stir in strawberry purée and vanilla. Cover and refrigerate until completely cold or overnight.

5. Stir milk mixture. Transfer to an ice cream maker and freeze according to manufacturer's instructions.

> **VARIATION: *Strawberry Balsamic Gelato:*** *Balsamic vinegar splashed on strawberries is a wonderful surprise. The same can be said for the above recipe when you stir in 1 tbsp (15 mL) aged balsamic vinegar along with the strawberry purée.*

# Vanilla Gelato

**SERVES 4 TO 6**

*On a hot summer day in Italy, you'll find most people leisurely licking a gelato. If you're going to make gelato from scratch, go for vanilla. But don't try to substitute something lighter for the whipping cream. As this gelato doesn't have an egg-custard base, we found that whipping cream made it rich and smooth. It's an easy recipe that's very satisfying — and one with many add-in possibilities.*

| | | |
|---|---|---|
| I | vanilla bean | I |
| 2 cups | milk | 500 mL |
| I cup | whipping (35%) cream | 250 mL |
| ¾ cup | granulated sugar | 175 mL |

**I.** Slit vanilla bean lengthwise and scrape seeds into a medium saucepan. Add vanilla pod, milk, cream and sugar. Place saucepan over medium-low heat. Cook, stirring occasionally, until sugar is dissolved. Bring to a simmer. Strain into a clean large bowl, discarding vanilla pod. Let cool to room temperature.

**2.** Cover and refrigerate until completely cold or overnight.

**3.** Stir cream mixture. Transfer to an ice cream maker and freeze according to manufacturer's instructions.

> **VARIATION:** *Chocolate Almond Gelato: Add* ½ *cup (125 mL) chocolate-covered almonds in the last 5 minutes of freezing and let machine stir them in.*

# Zabaglione Gelato

**SERVES 6**

*Zabaglione is an Italian egg custard kissed with Marsala wine and served warm. This frozen version will become a favorite dessert, particularly when it's paired with biscotti and a cup of espresso. You'll need either a double boiler to make this effectively or one stainless-steel bowl for the mixing that can safely be placed over a pot of simmering water.*

| | | |
|---|---|---|
| 2 cups | milk | 500 mL |
| 4 | egg yolks | 4 |
| 1/2 cup | granulated sugar | 125 mL |
| 1/3 cup | Marsala wine | 75 mL |
| 1 tbsp | lemon zest | 15 mL |

1. In the top half of a double boiler without the heat on, combine milk, egg yolks and sugar, stirring, until thoroughly blended.

2. Place top half of double boiler over bottom saucepan of simmering water. Whisk for 3 minutes or until thickened. Add Marsala wine and lemon zest and continue whisking for a few minutes more.

3. Remove top half of double boiler from bottom. Strain into a clean large bowl. Let cool to room temperature. Cover and refrigerate until completely cold or overnight.

4. Transfer to an ice cream maker and freeze according to manufacturer's instructions.

---

**VARIATION:** *You can make a Spanish-inspired gelato by substituting amontillado sherry for the Marsala wine and, at the last minute, adding 1 tbsp (15 mL) orange zest and 1/2 tsp (2 mL) ground cinnamon along with the lemon zest.*

# Ices, Sorbets & Granitas

# Apple Muscat Ice

**SERVES 6**

**Serving suggestion:** This is a great light dessert to complement a cheese-and-fruit platter.

*This idea came to us from Jacques and Lynn Bernier, who remember it as an all-time favorite. To ensure this tantalizing ice achieves a stable frozen state, we recommend that you make it with a low-alcohol Muscat wine, such as the 5.5% alcohol Moscato D'Asti. This is definitely a festive ice, perfect for entertaining and suitable as either a palate cleanser between courses or a frozen accompaniment to either fresh fruit or something devilishly chocolate. You may even choose to grate the apples unpeeled for extra color.*

| | | |
|---|---|---|
| 3 | Granny Smith apples, peeled and grated | 3 |
| 1 tbsp | freshly squeezed lemon juice | 15 mL |
| 1 cup | Simple Syrup (see recipe, page 23) | 250 mL |
| 1 cup | low-alcohol Muscat wine | 250 mL |
| 2 tbsp | liquid honey | 25 mL |
| 1/2 tsp | grated gingerroot | 2 mL |

1. In a bowl, toss apples with lemon juice. Stir in syrup, wine, honey and ginger. Cover and refrigerate until completely cold or overnight.

2. Stir apple mixture. Transfer to an ice cream maker and freeze according to manufacturer's instructions.

# Beet Apple Slush

**SERVES 4 TO 6**

**Serving suggestion:**
Garnish with a
dollop of sweetened
sour cream and
chopped fresh mint.

*Beets would seem an unlikely choice for a palate cleanser, but this delicious,
simple recipe is refreshing between courses or as a summertime starter.
You can use freshly squeezed beet juice or bottled — either will work fine.
A word to the wise: where there are beets, there are bound to be stains.*

| | | |
|---|---|---|
| 2 cups | beet juice | 500 mL |
| 1 cup | apple juice | 250 mL |
| 1/4 cup | granulated sugar | 50 mL |

1. In a bowl, stir together beet juice, apple juice and sugar until sugar is dissolved. Cover and refrigerate until completely cold or overnight.

2. Stir juice mixture. Transfer to an ice cream maker and freeze according to manufacturer's instructions.

# Berry Spiced Tea Ice

*When berries are abundant, combine them with tea and spices for an exotic and sophisticated twist. Use a full-bodied tea, such as oolong.*

**SERVES 4**

| | | |
|---|---|---|
| I cup | blackberries | 250 mL |
| I cup | Simple Syrup (see recipe, page 23) | 250 mL |
| ½ cup | raspberries | 125 mL |
| ½ cup | cold strong tea | 125 mL |
| I tbsp | freshly squeezed lemon juice | 15 mL |
| ½ tsp | ground cinnamon | 2 mL |
| Pinch | ground nutmeg | Pinch |
| Pinch | freshly ground black pepper | Pinch |

1. In a food processor or blender, purée blackberries, syrup, raspberries and tea until smooth. Using the back of a wooden spoon, press through a fine sieve into a bowl to remove seeds.

2. Stir in lemon juice, cinnamon, nutmeg and pepper. Cover and refrigerate until completely cold or overnight.

3. Stir berry mixture. Transfer to an ice cream maker and freeze according to manufacturer's instructions.

# Blackberry Cabernet Ice

**SERVES 6**

*This simple-to-make ice, with its deep color, is exquisite to look at and perfect for elegant dining during the summer, when these fruits are at their most luscious. You can use any full-bodied dry red wine and increase the amount of wine slightly — just remember that the more alcohol you add the less the ice will freeze.*

| | | |
|---|---|---|
| 3 cups | fresh blackberries | 750 mL |
| 2 cups | Simple Syrup (see recipe, page 23) | 500 mL |
| ¼ cup | Cabernet Sauvignon wine | 50 mL |
| 1 tsp | freshly squeezed lemon juice | 5 mL |

**1.** In a food processor or blender, in batches if necessary, purée blackberries, syrup, wine and lemon juice until smooth. Using the back of a wooden spoon, press through a fine sieve into a bowl to remove seeds. Cover and refrigerate until completely cold or overnight.

**2.** Stir berry mixture. Transfer to an ice cream maker and freeze according to manufacturer's instructions.

**VARIATION:** *Blueberry Zinfandel Ice: Substitute blueberries for the blackberries and white Zinfandel for the Cabernet Sauvignon.*

# Blood Orange Ice

**SERVES 6 TO 8**

*The fruit that gets its name from its purplish-red flesh produces an easy-to-make ice of incredible sophistication and flavor. Though grown primarily in Mediterranean countries, blood oranges are usually available in North America from late winter to early spring and are sometimes labeled "ruby oranges." For an additional zing, add $1/4$ cup (50 mL) Cabernet Sauvignon wine or Campari while you're puréeing the fruit.*

| 8 | large blood oranges | 8 |
|---|---|---|
| I cup | Simple Syrup (see recipe, page 23) | 250 mL |
| | Juice of $1/2$ lime, about 2 tbsp (25 mL) | |

1. Peel blood oranges, being careful to remove all of the rind and the white pith beneath.

2. In a food processor or blender, purée blood oranges with syrup until smooth. Using the back of a wooden spoon, press through a fine sieve into a bowl to remove seeds. Stir in lime juice. Cover and refrigerate until completely cold or overnight.

3. Stir juice mixture. Transfer to an ice cream maker and freeze according to manufacturer's instructions.

# Blueberry Ginger Ice

**SERVES 4**

**Tip:** When using herbs, make sure they have not been treated with pesticides. Treat herbs to a light wash in soapy water and rinse very well.

*It seems not to matter whether you use fresh or thawed frozen blueberries in this recipe. You can omit the chopped mint if you prefer. For a perfect red-white-and-blue holiday dessert, serve a scoop of this ice with a scoop of vanilla ice cream and a scoop of raspberry ice.*

| | | |
|---|---|---|
| 2 cups | blueberries | 500 mL |
| 1 cup | Simple Syrup (see recipe, page 23) | 250 mL |
| 2 tbsp | grated gingerroot | 25 mL |
| 2 tbsp | freshly squeezed lime juice | 25 mL |
| 1 tbsp | finely chopped fresh mint (see Tip, left) | 15 mL |
| 1 tbsp | freshly squeezed lemon juice | 15 mL |

1. In a food processor or blender, purée blueberries, syrup, ginger, lime juice, mint and lemon juice until smooth. Transfer to a bowl. Cover and refrigerate until completely cold or overnight.

2. Stir berry mixture. Transfer to an ice cream maker and freeze according to manufacturer's instructions.

**VARIATION:** *Blueberry Ginger Zinfandel Ice:* Add 1/2 cup (125 mL) white Zinfandel wine to mixture before chilling.

# Cantaloupe Ice

**SERVES 6 TO 8**

*This works best with very ripe cantaloupe, but you can also use honeydew melon. If you want to pair melon with another fruit, blueberry works particularly well; just add $\frac{1}{2}$ cup (125 mL) fresh blueberries to the food processor along with the melon.*

| | | |
|---|---|---|
| I | large ripe cantaloupe, peeled, seeded and chopped (about 8 cups/2 L) | I |
| I cup | Simple Syrup (see recipe, page 23) | 250 mL |
| $\frac{1}{4}$ cup | orange juice | 50 mL |
| $\frac{1}{4}$ cup | freshly squeezed lemon juice | 50 mL |

1. In a food processor or blender, purée cantaloupe, syrup, orange juice and lemon juice until smooth. Transfer to a bowl. Cover and refrigerate until completely cold or overnight.

2. Stir cantaloupe mixture. Transfer to an ice cream maker and freeze according to manufacturer's instructions.

# Carrot Ice

**SERVES 6 TO 8**

*Save those carrot sticks for lunch boxes and try serving this as a palate cleanser at an adult party. Or, topped with chopped crystallized ginger, serve it as a memorable and fine finish to a more formal occasion. You can purchase carrot juice at health-food stores or you can make your own with a juicer.*

| | | |
|---|---|---|
| 3 cups | carrot juice | 750 mL |
| I | small carrot, grated | I |
| ½ cup | Simple Syrup (see recipe, page 23) | 125 mL |
| ¼ cup | apple juice | 50 mL |
| I tsp | grated lemon zest | 5 mL |
| I tbsp | freshly squeezed lemon juice | 25 mL |

**1.** In a bowl, stir together carrot juice, carrot, syrup, apple juice and lemon zest and juice until combined. Cover and refrigerate until completely cold or overnight.

**2.** Stir carrot mixture. Transfer to an ice cream maker and freeze according to manufacturer's instructions.

# Chocolate Ice

**SERVES 4**

*This is a good example of how a recipe is so much more than just the sum of its parts. The ingredients would seem to add up to frozen chocolate water, but the result is an exquisite dessert that you will make over and over again. The trick is the quality of chocolate used — we used Lindt 70% dark chocolate — so don't make this with the traditional baking variety.*

| | | |
|---|---|---|
| 1/2 cup | granulated sugar | 125 mL |
| 1/4 cup | unsweetened cocoa powder | 50 mL |
| 3 oz | bittersweet chocolate, finely chopped | 90 g |
| 1 tbsp | orange zest | 15 mL |
| 1/4 cup | freshly squeezed orange juice | 50 mL |

1. In a medium saucepan over medium heat, bring 2 cups (500 mL) water, sugar and cocoa powder to a boil, whisking constantly.

2. Reduce heat and simmer for 1 minute or until sugar is dissolved and cocoa is well blended. Stir in chopped chocolate until melted. Remove from heat and transfer to a bowl. Let cool to room temperature.

3. Stir in orange zest and juice. Cover and refrigerate until completely cold or overnight.

4. Stir chocolate mixture. Transfer to an ice cream maker and freeze according to manufacturer's instructions.

Grape Gelato (page 109)
*Overleaf:* Mango Ginger Coulis (page 177)
and Hot Butterscotch Sauce (page 175)

# Coffee Granita

**SERVES 6 TO 8**

*This is the classic Italian slushy, usually served in a tall glass and topped with whipped cream. Granitas are frozen desserts made in the freezer by hand, not in an ice cream machine. It seems daunting but is really easy to do and worth the extra bit of work.*

13-BY 9-INCH (3 L) METAL BAKING PAN

| 4 cups | freshly brewed strong coffee | 1 L |
|--------|------------------------------|--------|
| 1 cup | granulated sugar | 250 mL |
| | Zest of 1 lemon | |
| 1 tsp | vanilla | 5 mL |
| 2 | whole star anise | 2 |

1. In a bowl, stir together coffee, sugar, lemon zest, vanilla and star anise until sugar is dissolved. Let cool to room temperature.

2. Discard star anise. Pour into baking pan. Freeze for about 1 hour or until ice forms at the edges of the pan.

3. Using a fork, break up ice and stir to distribute frozen portions evenly. Freeze for 30 minutes or until solid.

4. Using a fork, stir to break up ice crystals. Continue freezing, stirring the mixture every 20 minutes, until slushy. Serve with whipped cream.

Persimmon Gelato (page 114)

# Cranberry Sorbet

**SERVES 4 TO 6**

*This sorbet is a little more substantial than ones traditionally made with just cranberry juice. If you want to cut down on the calories, you can use artificially sweetened juice instead of the Simple Syrup. If you cut back on the sugar syrup and increase the lemon juice to taste, you can concoct a lively palate-cleansing ice for a formal Christmas or New Year's dinner.*

| | | |
|---|---|---|
| 2 cups | unsweetened cranberry juice | 500 mL |
| ½ cup | dried cranberries | 125 mL |
| 1 cup | Simple Syrup (see recipe, page 23) | 250 mL |
| ¼ cup | orange juice | 50 mL |
| 1 tbsp | freshly squeezed lemon juice | 15 mL |

1. In a bowl, stir cranberry juice with dried cranberries. Let stand for 1 hour or until cranberries are plump.

2. Stir in syrup, orange juice and lemon juice. Cover and refrigerate until completely cold or overnight.

3. Stir cranberry mixture. Transfer to an ice cream maker and freeze according to manufacturer's instructions.

# Cuban Ice

*This is our version of the* mojito, *the classic Cuban cocktail. Serve it as a starter, a palate cleanser or a light dessert for a Latin-themed dinner.*

**SERVES 4**

| | | |
|---|---|---|
| 2 cups | Simple Syrup (see recipe, page 23) | 500 mL |
| | Juice of 2 limes | |
| ½ cup | white rum | 125 mL |
| ¼ cup | chopped fresh mint (see Tip, page 125) | 50 mL |

1. In a bowl, stir together syrup, lime juice and rum. Cover and refrigerate until completely cold or overnight.

2. Stir syrup mixture. Transfer to an ice cream maker and freeze according to manufacturer's instructions. Garnish each serving with mint.

# Kiwi Banana Lime Ice

**SERVES 6 TO 8**

*The addition of a banana makes this a very agreeable combination that has the consistency of ice cream — without the fat.*

| 2 cups | Simple Syrup (see recipe, page 23) | 500 mL |
| 6 | kiwifruits, peeled and chopped (about 2 cups/500 mL) | 6 |
| 1 | large banana, sliced | 1 |
| 1 tbsp | freshly squeezed lime juice | 15 mL |

1. In a food processor or blender, purée syrup, kiwifruits, banana and lime juice until smooth. Transfer to a bowl. Cover and refrigerate until completely cold or overnight.

2. Stir fruit mixture. Transfer to an ice cream maker and freeze according to manufacturer's instructions.

# Lime Granita

**SERVES 4 TO 6**

*More sour than sweet, this granita is incredibly refreshing on a hot summer day. A little bit of it is also excellent as a between-courses palate cleanser.*

13-BY 9-INCH (3 L) METAL BAKING PAN

| | | |
|---|---|---|
| 2 cups | water | 500 mL |
| I cup | granulated sugar | 250 mL |
| | Zest of I lime | |
| I cup | freshly squeezed lime juice | 250 mL |

1. In a bowl, stir together water, sugar, lime zest and juice until sugar is dissolved.

2. Pour into metal baking pan and freeze for I hour or until ice forms at the edges of the pan.

3. Using a fork, break up ice and stir to distribute frozen portions evenly. Freeze for 30 minutes or until solid.

4. Using a fork, stir to break up ice crystals. Continue freezing, stirring the mixture every 20 minutes, until slushy.

# Lychee Ice

**SERVES 4 TO 6**

*Even if you'd never think of peeling your own fresh lychees, you'll love this exotic ice. Instead of fresh fruit, it's made with lychees canned in syrup that are available in most supermarkets or any Asian grocery store. For an extra-special twist, add ½ cup (125 mL) chopped crystallized ginger in the last 5 minutes of freezing. Or serve as is with the chopped ginger on top.*

| | | |
|---|---|---|
| 1 | can (19 oz/540 mL) lychees in syrup | 1 |
| 1 cup | apple juice | 250 mL |
| 1 tbsp | freshly squeezed lime juice | 15 mL |

1. In a food processor or blender, purée lychees with syrup until smooth.

2. Transfer to a bowl. Stir in apple juice and lime juice. Cover and refrigerate until completely cold or overnight.

3. Stir lychee mixture. Transfer to an ice cream maker and freeze according to manufacturer's instructions.

# Mandarin Orange Ice

**SERVES 6 TO 8**

*This is a quick, refreshing dessert to serve after a substantial meal. We make it during those months when mandarin oranges are not available fresh. Serve a scoop of it on a slice of dense chocolate cake.*

| 4 | cans (each 10 oz/284 mL) mandarin oranges in syrup | 4 |
| --- | --- | --- |
| 1/2 cup | granulated sugar | 125 mL |
| 1/4 cup | freshly squeezed lemon juice | 50 mL |

1. In a food processor or blender, purée oranges with syrup, sugar and lemon juice until smooth. Transfer to a bowl. Cover and refrigerate until completely cold or overnight.

2. Stir orange mixture. Transfer to an ice cream maker and freeze according to manufacturer's instructions.

# Mango Ginger Ice

*You can use 3 cups (750 mL) chopped fresh mango for this recipe, but the canned fruit works equally well.*

**SERVES 6 TO 8**

| | | |
|---|---|---|
| I cup | Simple Syrup (see recipe, page 23) | 250 mL |
| I | large ripe banana, sliced | I |
| 2 | cans (each 14 oz/398 mL) mango in syrup | 2 |
| I tsp | grated gingerroot | 5 mL |

1. In a food processor or blender, purée syrup, banana, mango with syrup and ginger until smooth. Transfer to a bowl. Cover and refrigerate until completely cold or overnight.

2. Stir mango mixture. Transfer to an ice cream maker and freeze according to manufacturer's instructions.

# Papaya Ice

*Make sure you use only the ripest papayas for this refreshing recipe, which has the consistency of ice cream, thanks to the addition of a banana. This is a terrific dessert for a hot, steamy day. Serve with crisp shortbreads or gingersnaps on the side.*

| 2 cups | chopped ripe papaya | 500 mL |
|--------|---------------------|--------|
| 1 cup | Simple Syrup (see recipe, page 23) | 250 mL |
| 1 | large ripe banana, sliced | 1 |
| | Juice of 2 limes | |

1. In a food processor or blender, purée papaya, syrup, banana and lime juice until smooth. Transfer to a bowl. Cover and refrigerate until completely cold or overnight.

2. Stir papaya mixture. Transfer to an ice cream maker and freeze according to manufacturer's instructions.

---

**VARIATION:** *You can develop your own version by playing with flavors and combinations. For example, instead of 2 cups (500 mL) chopped papaya, try 1 cup (250 mL) chopped papaya and 1 cup (250 mL) chopped mango.*

# Pear Cardamom Sorbet

**SERVES 8**

*Cardamom, a spice popular in Indian cuisine, is paired with pears for a unique, agreeable taste. We especially recommend this ice after a meal of curry. Because we use canned pears, this sorbet is easy to make any time of year.*

**Serving suggestion:** The French term *trou normand* is roughly translated as "Norman hole" and is popular in the region of Normandy as a dessert sorbet splashed with an *eau-de-vie*. To make your own, use the bottom of a coffee spoon to press a hole into the center of a scoop of Pear Cardamom Sorbet, then fill the hole with a pear *eau-de-vie* or brandy of your choice.

| | | |
|---|---|---|
| 1 cup | Simple Syrup (see recipe, page 23) | 250 mL |
| 2 | cans (each 14 oz/398 mL) pears in syrup | 2 |
| 2 tbsp | freshly squeezed lemon juice | 25 mL |
| Pinch | ground cardamom | Pinch |

1. In a food processor or blender, purée syrup, pears with syrup, lemon juice and cardamom until smooth. Transfer to a bowl. Cover and refrigerate until completely cold or overnight.

2. Stir pear mixture. Transfer to an ice cream maker and freeze according to manufacturer's instructions.

> **VARIATION:** *Pear Ginger Sorbet: Substitute 2 tbsp (25 mL) finely chopped crystallized ginger for the cardamom.*

# Pear Cranberry Ice

**SERVES 6**

**Tip:** This recipe doubles well if you're making it for a larger group of guests or want extra on hand for the family.

*We used canned pears for this easy dessert that celebrates winter and illustrates that cranberries are worth getting to know beyond Thanksgiving and Christmas. You can even omit the fresh cranberries and the honey for an easier "cupboard" version.*

| | | |
|---|---|---:|
| 1 cup | water | 250 mL |
| $\frac{1}{2}$ cup | fresh cranberries | 125 mL |
| 1 | can (14 oz/398 mL) pear halves in syrup | 1 |
| $1\frac{1}{2}$ cups | cranberry juice | 375 mL |
| 1 tbsp | liquid honey | 15 mL |

1. In a medium saucepan over high heat, cook water and fresh cranberries until the cranberries pop. Let cool.

2. In a food processor, purée pears with syrup until smooth.

3. Add cranberry mixture, cranberry juice and honey. Pulse for 30 seconds. Transfer to a clean large bowl. Cover and refrigerate until completely cold or overnight.

4. Stir pear mixture. Transfer to an ice cream maker and freeze according to manufacturer's instructions.

**VARIATION:** *If you prefer a taste that is more pear than cranberry or vice versa, play with the amounts. For a more intense pear flavor, use 2 cans of pears in syrup; for a more cranberry taste, double the amount of fresh cranberries to 1 cup (250 mL). Proceed with the recipe.*

# Pineapple Rum Ice

**SERVES 4**

*This ice is perfect for a Caribbean-themed party where you serve jerk chicken and black beans and rice.*

| | | |
|---|---|---|
| 2 cups | fresh pineapple chunks | 500 mL |
| 1 cup | Simple Syrup (see recipe, page 23) | 250 mL |
| ½ | large ripe banana, sliced | ½ |
| 1 tbsp | dark rum | 15 mL |

1. In a food processor or blender, purée pineapple, syrup, banana and rum until smooth. Transfer to a bowl. Cover and refrigerate until completely cold or overnight.

2. Stir fruit mixture. Transfer to an ice cream maker and freeze according to manufacturer's instructions.

# Pineapple Star Anise Ice

SERVES 4

*Truly exotic is the licorice-like taste of pretty star-shaped anise pods, which are popular in Chinese cooking. Serve with grilled or roasted pineapple slices or over old-fashioned pineapple upside-down cake.*

| | | |
|---|---|---|
| 1 cup | Simple Syrup (see recipe, page 23) | 250 mL |
| 4 | whole star anise | 4 |
| 2 cups | fresh pineapple chunks | 500 mL |
| 1 tbsp | freshly squeezed lemon juice | 15 mL |

1. In a medium saucepan, bring syrup and star anise to a boil. Reduce heat and simmer for 5 minutes. Let cool to room temperature. Discard star anise.

2. In a food processor or blender, purée syrup mixture, pineapple and lemon juice until smooth. Transfer to a bowl. Cover and refrigerate until completely cold or overnight.

3. Stir pineapple mixture. Transfer to an ice cream maker and freeze according to manufacturer's instructions.

# Pink Grapefruit Star Anise Ice

*Think pink for a wonderfully refreshing ice that's a perfect palate refresher or a welcome dessert. The star anise gives it an exotic edge.*

**SERVES 8 TO 10**

**Tips:** To get the required fresh grapefruit juice, you'll need 3 to 4 pink grapefruits, seeds removed.

Serve this ice in champagne flutes, topped with a few raspberries and chopped fresh mint.

| | | |
|---|---|---|
| 2 cups | water | 500 mL |
| 1⅓ cups | granulated sugar | 325 mL |
| 3 | whole star anise | 3 |
| 4 cups | freshly squeezed pink grapefruit juice (see Tips, left) | 1 L |

1. In a medium saucepan, bring water, sugar and star anise to a boil. Cook, stirring, until sugar is dissolved. Remove from heat and let stand for 15 minutes. Discard star anise. Let cool.

2. Stir juice into sugar mixture. Transfer to a clean large bowl. Cover and refrigerate until completely cold or overnight.

3. Stir juice mixture. Transfer to an ice cream maker and freeze according to manufacturer's instructions.

# Santa Fe Raspberry Lime Ice

**SERVES 4**

**Tip:** Pickled jalapeños work just fine in this recipe. If you're using a fresh pepper, use a medium-hot pepper and wear kitchen gloves to avoid burning your skin. Remove the seeds and ribs, then chop finely.

**Serving suggestion:** Serve Santa Fe Raspberry Lime Ice in a martini glass rimmed with tequila and granulated sugar.

*This ice, with its flavor of berries enriched with a hit of lime, shakes up your taste buds and the conversation with its Southwest nod to the chili pepper. Enjoy it as a palate cleanser between courses or as a dessert paired with chocolate chip cookies or brownies. Tone down the fire, stoke it up or leave the pepper out altogether.*

| | | |
|---|---|---|
| 1 1/2 cups | raspberries, fresh or frozen | 375 mL |
| 1 cup | Simple Syrup (see recipe, page 23) | 250 mL |
| | Zest and juice of 2 limes | |
| 1/2 tsp | finely chopped jalapeño pepper (see Tip, left) | 2 mL |

1. In a food processor or blender, purée raspberries with syrup until smooth.

2. Using the back of a wooden spoon, press through a fine sieve into a bowl to remove seeds. Stir in lime zest and juice and jalapeño pepper. Cover and refrigerate until completely cold or overnight.

3. Stir raspberry mixture. Transfer to an ice cream maker and freeze according to manufacturer's instructions.

> **VARIATION:** *Minty Raspberry Lime Ice:* To capture the essence of summer, replace the pepper with 2 tbsp (25 mL) chopped fresh mint.

# Spiced Wine Sorbet

**SERVES 6 TO 8**

**Tip:** Even though
you reduce the
liquid, and thereby
cook off much
of the alcohol,
we found that this
sorbet doesn't freeze
as well as some.
This doesn't detract
from its enjoyment
though. It's a
winner, for sure!

*Anyone who loves mulled wine will enjoy it in frozen form. We like
to serve it with honeyed oranges on the side as a heady finish to a dinner
of roast lamb.*

| | | |
|---|---|---|
| I | bottle (28 oz/750 mL) dry red wine | I |
| I cup | granulated sugar | 250 mL |
| I cup | apple juice | 250 mL |
| I | lemon, sliced | I |
| I | orange, sliced | I |
| 3 | cinnamon sticks, broken in half | 3 |
| IO | whole cloves | IO |
| IO | whole black peppercorns | IO |
| ½ tsp | ground allspice | 2 mL |

1. In a large saucepan, bring all the ingredients to a boil.
   Reduce heat to medium and cook until reduced by
   one-third, about 15 minutes. Remove from heat and
   let cool.

2. Strain into a clean large bowl. Cover and refrigerate until
   completely cold or overnight.

3. Stir wine mixture. Transfer to an ice cream maker and
   freeze according to manufacturer's instructions.

# Strawberry Pineapple Sorbet

*Try this low-calorie fruity sorbet, especially if you or your guests are on a sugar-restricted diet.*

**SERVES 4 TO 6**

| | | |
|---|---|---|
| 3 cups | chopped strawberries | 750 mL |
| ¾ cup | pineapple juice | 175 mL |
| ½ | large banana | ½ |

1. In a food processor or blender, purée strawberries, pineapple juice, banana and ¼ cup (50 mL) water until smooth. Transfer to a bowl. Cover and refrigerate until completely cold or overnight.

2. Stir fruit mixture. Transfer to an ice cream maker and freeze according to manufacturer's instructions.

# Tequila Orange Granita

**SERVES 6**

*Great for a Mexican-themed party, this citrus-flavored granita can work not only as a refreshing dessert but also as a fun way to begin the party.*

13-BY 9-INCH (3 L) METAL BAKING PAN

| | | |
|---|---|---|
| $1/2$ cup | granulated sugar | 125 mL |
| | Juice of 7 oranges | |
| | (about $2^1/3$ cups/575 mL) | |
| 6 tbsp | white tequila | 90 mL |
| 6 | slices lime | 6 |

1. In a bowl, stir together $1^1/4$ cups (300 mL) water, sugar, orange juice and tequila until sugar is dissolved.

2. Pour into baking pan and freeze for about 1 hour or until ice forms at the edges of the pan.

3. Using a fork, break up ice and stir to distribute frozen portions evenly. Freeze for 30 minutes or until solid.

4. Using a fork, stir to break up ice crystals. Continue freezing, stirring the mixture every 20 minutes, until slushy. Garnish with lime slices.

# Tomato Basil Ice

**SERVES 8 TO 10**

*This ice is a welcome first course during a heat wave. Serve it on its own or dollop it in chilled corn or cucumber soup. For the best flavor, wait until tomatoes are at their ripest.*

| | | |
|---|---|---|
| 5 | large ripe tomatoes (about 3 lbs/1.5 kg) | 5 |
| ½ cup | tomato juice | 125 mL |
| ¼ cup | chopped fresh basil leaves (see Tip, page 125) | 50 mL |
| ¼ cup | freshly squeezed lemon juice | 50 mL |
| 2 tbsp | tomato paste | 25 mL |
| 1 tbsp | olive oil | 15 mL |
| | Salt and freshly ground black pepper | |

1. Peel, core and seed tomatoes. Chop.

2. In a food processor or blender, purée tomatoes, tomato juice, basil, lemon juice, tomato paste and oil until smooth. Transfer to a bowl. Add salt and pepper to taste. Cover and refrigerate until completely cold or overnight.

3. Stir tomato mixture. Transfer to an ice cream maker and freeze according to manufacturer's instructions.

# Watermelon Frozen Margaritas

*We call this updated cocktail of the '90s The Adult Slushy. With this much liquor in it, it won't freeze completely, so it's best enjoyed in slush form straight from the ice cream maker.*

**SERVES 6 TO 8**

**Tip:** You can decrease the Simple Syrup to ¼ cup (50 mL) if you prefer your margaritas less sweet.

**Serving suggestion:** Rub the rim of a glass with lime, then dip in salt. Fill with slushy Watermelon Frozen Margarita and serve with a thick straw.

| | | |
|---|---|---|
| 5 cups | chopped seeded watermelon | 1.25 L |
| ½ cup | Simple Syrup (see recipe, page 23) | 125 mL |
| ½ cup | freshly squeezed lime juice | 125 mL |
| ¾ cup | white tequila | 175 mL |

1. In a food processor or blender, purée watermelon, syrup and lime juice until smooth. Transfer to a bowl. Stir in tequila. Cover and refrigerate until completely cold or overnight.

2. Stir fruit mixture. Transfer to an ice cream maker and freeze according to manufacturer's instructions.

> **VARIATION:** *Frozen Watermelon Mojitos: Substitute dark rum for the tequila. Add 2 tbsp (25 mL) chopped fresh mint.*

# Watermelon Lemonade Ice

**SERVES 4**

**Tip:** To make ice pops, divide mixture among 8 ice-pop molds. Cover and freeze until firm.

*Scrape this frozen ice into a slushie on a hot day. Or try it frozen solid in ice-pop molds (see Tip, left).*

13-BY 9-INCH (3 L) METAL BAKING PAN

| 2 cups | finely chopped seeded watermelon | 500 mL |
| 1 cup | frozen lemonade concentrate, thawed | 250 mL |

1. In a food processor or blender, purée watermelon with lemonade concentrate until smooth.

2. Pour into baking pan and freeze for 1 hour or until ice forms at the edges of the pan.

3. Using a fork, break up ice and stir to distribute frozen portions evenly. Freeze for 30 minutes or until solid.

# Watermelon Mint Ice

**SERVES 4 TO 6**

*You can make this with red or yellow watermelon. The addition of orange and lime juices gives the recipe an even-more-tropical flavor. You can also serve this when it's slushy, just before it freezes, for a treat that kids especially will love!*

| | | |
|---|---|---|
| 2 cups | chopped seeded watermelon | 500 mL |
| 1 cup | Simple Syrup (see recipe, page 23) | 250 mL |
| ½ cup | orange juice | 125 mL |
| 1 tbsp | freshly squeezed lime juice | 15 mL |
| 1 tbsp | finely chopped fresh mint (see Tip, page 125) | 15 mL |

1. In a food processor or blender, purée watermelon, syrup, orange juice, lime juice and mint until smooth. Transfer to a bowl. Cover and refrigerate until completely cold or overnight.

2. Stir fruit mixture. Transfer to an ice cream maker and freeze according to manufacturer's instructions.

# DRINKS & ICE POPS

# Cocktail Pops

**SERVES 6**

**Tip:** To unmold, immerse the bottom of the ice-cube tray in warm water for 30 seconds.

*Who says finger foods always have to be savory? These one-bite ice creams are a great way to add a memorable moment to any party. The more flavorful the ice cream the better: choose Pumpkin Ice Cream (page 90), Pucker-Up Ice Cream (page 89), Ginger Ice Cream (page 59) or Chocolate Mousse Ice Cream (page 45) — or make a variety of flavors so guests can choose.*

**LARGE ICE-CUBE TRAY**

> Assorted ice cream flavors
> Popsicle sticks, lemongrass spears
> or cinnamon sticks

**1.** Press ice cream into ice-cube molds. Insert sticks.

**2.** Freeze until firm.

**3.** Unmold just before serving.

# Coffee Frappé

**SERVES 4**

*Ice-blended creamy coffee beverages are sweeping the country. Here's our version to be served in coffee cups. A splash of coffee liqueur over each serving is optional.*

| | | |
|---|---|---|
| 8 | scoops coffee ice cream, such as Café au Lait (see recipe, page 33) | 8 |
| 2 cups | crushed ice | 500 mL |
| I cup | cold espresso | 250 mL |
| | Ground cinnamon to taste | |

1. In a food processor or blender, purée half of the coffee ice cream, the ice and espresso until smooth.

2. Pour into four cups or glasses. Top each with one scoop of the remaining ice cream and sprinkle with cinnamon.

# Gin Fizz

**SERVES 6**

**Serving suggestion:**
Rim each glass
with lemon then
dip in sugar.

*Gin and tonic is a popular happy-hour standby. This fruity version,
meant to be eaten as well as sipped, is a welcome alternative as a
late-afternoon adult pick-me-up.*

| | | |
|---|---|---|
| I cup | mixed berries, fresh or frozen | 250 mL |
| I tbsp | lemon zest | 15 mL |
| ¼ cup | freshly squeezed lemon juice | 50 mL |
| 4 | scoops Lime Granita (see recipe, page 133) | 4 |
| ½ cup | gin | 125 mL |
| I cup | tonic water | 250 mL |

1. In a bowl, toss together berries and lemon zest and juice.

2. Divide berry mixture among four tall glasses. Add one
scoop Lime Granita to each.

3. Divide gin among glasses. Top with tonic water.

# Hot Chocolate with Cold Center

SERVES 4

*This is a perfect treat to enjoy on a chilly autumn afternoon after a few hours of yardwork. If you prefer, substitute your favorite powdered hot chocolate mix for the grated semisweet.*

| 2 cups | skim milk | 500 mL |
|--------|-----------|--------|
| 6 oz | semisweet chocolate, chopped | 175 g |
| 4 | scoops chocolate ice cream | 4 |
| | Grated semisweet chocolate | |

1. In a medium saucepan over medium heat, heat milk with chopped chocolate, stirring, until chocolate is melted and mixture is smooth and steaming.

2. Divide ice cream among four mugs. Pour milk mixture over top. Top with grated chocolate.

# Lemon Martini
# Ice Pops

**SERVES 6**

*Plastic ice-pop molds are easy to find in the supermarket and are inexpensive, so you can experiment well beyond the traditional lemonade or orange juice pops. We especially like this adult martini version. Because of its liquid consistency, we recommend waiting until the mixture is semifrozen before inserting the sticks.*

ICE-POP MOLD
POPSICLE STICKS

| | | |
|---|---|---|
| 1/4 cup | granulated sugar | 50 mL |
| | Zest of 1 lemon | |
| 1/4 cup | gin | 50 mL |
| 3 tbsp | dry vermouth | 45 mL |

1. In a medium saucepan over medium heat, heat 1 1/2 cups (375 mL) water with sugar, stirring, until sugar is dissolved. Let cool to room temperature.

2. Transfer to a bowl. Stir in lemon zest, gin and vermouth. Cover and refrigerate until completely cold or overnight.

3. Stir syrup mixture. Pour into ice-pop molds and freeze until slushy. Insert sticks. Return to freezer and freeze until firm.

---

**VARIATION:** *Crantini Ice Pops: Substitute 1 3/4 cups (425 mL) cranberry juice for water and sugar. Add lemon, gin and vermouth and freeze as directed.*

# Lemony Float

*This summer treat is a good way to get your ice cream fix without wrestling with a messy cone. It's perfect for long, slow sipping by a cool northern lake.*

| | | |
|---|---|---|
| 2 cups | cold lemonade | 250 mL |
| 2 | large scoops ice cream, such as Old-Fashioned Vanilla Ice Cream (see recipe, page 80), Pucker-Up Ice Cream (see recipe, page 89) or Ginger Ice Cream (see recipe, page 59) Chopped fresh mint leaves | 2 |

**1.** Pour lemonade into two tall glasses. Add one scoop of ice cream to each glass.

**2.** Garnish with mint.

# Raspberry Yogurt Ice Pops

**SERVES 2 OR 3**

Not only is this a healthy summer snack but it's also one that kids (and adults) are sure to love. You can use your favorite fresh berries in this. We love the taste of raspberries despite their seeds.

ICE-POP MOLDS
POPSICLE STICKS

| 2 cups | fresh raspberries | 500 mL |
| 1 cup | raspberry-flavored yogurt | 250 mL |
| 1/4 cup | liquid honey | 50 mL |
| 1 tsp | lemon zest | 5 mL |

1. In a food processor or blender, purée raspberries. (If desired, press the raspberry purée through a sieve into a bowl to remove seeds.)

2. In a bowl, combine raspberry purée with yogurt. Mix well. Stir in 1/2 cup (125 mL) water, honey and lemon zest.

3. Divide among ice-pop molds and freeze until slushy. Insert sticks. Return to freezer and freeze until firm.

---

**VARIATIONS:** *Peach Yogurt Ice Pops:* Substitute 2 cups (500 mL) chopped pitted peeled peaches for the raspberries, and peach-flavored yogurt for the raspberry-flavored yogurt.

*Kiwi Yogurt Ice Pops:* Substitute 2 cups (500 mL) chopped peeled kiwifruits for the raspberries, and plain yogurt for the raspberry-flavored yogurt.

# Low-Fat Ice Milks, Yogurts & Non-Dairy Desserts

# Banana Soy Freeze

**SERVES 2 OR 3**

*Today's soy beverages taste much better than those of a decade ago. This banana soy "ice cream" is perfect for people who have dairy allergies or who just want to get more beneficial soy into their diet.*

| | | |
|---|---|---|
| ½ cup | Simple Syrup (see recipe, page 23) | 125 mL |
| 1 tbsp | freshly squeezed lemon juice | 15 mL |
| 2 | large ripe bananas, sliced | 2 |
| 1½ cups | vanilla-flavored soy beverage | 375 mL |
| ¼ tsp | vanilla | 1 mL |

1. In a food processor or blender, purée syrup, lemon juice and bananas until smooth.

2. Transfer to a large bowl. Stir in soy beverage and vanilla. Cover and refrigerate until completely cold or overnight.

3. Stir banana mixture. Transfer to an ice cream maker and freeze according to manufacturer's instructions.

Peach Yogurt Ice Pops and Kiwi Yogurt Ice Pops
(see Variations, page 158)

# Chocolate Honey Low-Fat Frozen Yogurt

*Before serving, we transfer this from freezer to fridge for 15 minutes because the lack of fat produces a rock-solid, though delicious, dessert.*

**SERVES 4**

| | | |
|---|---|---|
| 1 | container (26 oz/750 g) plain non-fat yogurt | 1 |
| 1/3 cup | liquid honey | 75 mL |
| 1 tbsp | finely chopped bittersweet chocolate | 15 mL |

1. In a bowl, stir together yogurt, honey and chocolate. Cover and refrigerate until completely cold or overnight.

2. Stir yogurt mixture. Transfer to an ice cream maker and freeze according to manufacturer's instructions.

Raspberry Buttermilk Ice Cream (page 166)

# Chocolate Soy "Ice Cream"

**SERVES 2 OR 3**

*With so many soy beverages to choose from, you can easily make this mock ice cream at home. We used milk chocolate, but you can substitute shavings of your favorite bittersweet chocolate bar.*

| | | |
|---|---|---|
| 2 cups | chocolate-flavored soy beverage | 500 mL |
| 1 cup | Simple Syrup | 250 mL |
| | (see recipe, page 23) | |
| ¼ cup | shaved milk chocolate | 50 mL |
| 1 tsp | vanilla | 5 mL |

**1.** In a bowl, stir together soy beverage, syrup, shaved chocolate and vanilla until combined. Cover and refrigerate until completely cold or overnight.

**2.** Stir soy mixture. Transfer to an ice cream maker and freeze according to manufacturer's instructions.

# Fig and Tofu "Ice Cream"

*This "ice cream" is completely dairy-free. It's tasty and healthy and has all the creaminess of the real thing.*

**SERVES 2 OR 3**

| | | |
|---|---|---|
| 1 cup | dried figs | 250 mL |
| 1 cup | apple juice | 250 mL |
| ½ cup | cubed drained semi-firm tofu | 125 mL |
| ⅔ cup | unsweetened plain soy beverage | 150 mL |
| ½ tsp | ground cinnamon | 2 mL |

1. In a medium saucepan over medium heat, bring figs and apple juice to a simmer. Cook for 10 minutes, stirring occasionally. Remove from heat and let stand for 1 hour or until figs are plump.

2. In a food processor or blender, purée fig mixture with tofu until smooth.

3. Transfer to a bowl. Stir in soy beverage and cinnamon. Cover and refrigerate until completely cold or overnight.

4. Stir soy mixture. Transfer to an ice cream maker and freeze according to manufacturer's instructions.

# Orange
# Frozen Yogurt

**SERVES 4**

*Try this for breakfast with a side of sliced bananas and strawberries.*

| 2 | egg yolks | 2 |
|---|---|---|
| 1/3 cup | packed brown sugar | 75 mL |
| 1/2 cup | 2% milk | 125 mL |
| 1 1/4 cups | plain yogurt | 300 mL |
| 1 tbsp | orange zest | 15 mL |
| 1/4 cup | freshly squeezed orange juice | 50 mL |
| 1/4 cup | granola | 50 mL |

1. In a bowl, whisk egg yolks with sugar until thickened and pale yellow. Set aside.

2. In a medium saucepan over medium-low heat, heat milk until bubbles appear around the edge of pan. Gradually whisk into the egg mixture.

3. Return the entire mixture to the saucepan. Cook over low heat, stirring constantly, until the mixture is thick enough to coat the back of a wooden spoon. Be careful not to let it boil. Strain into a clean large bowl. Let cool to room temperature.

4. Cover and refrigerate until completely cold or overnight.

5. Stir in yogurt, orange zest and juice. Transfer to an ice cream maker and freeze according to manufacturer's instructions.

6. Serve sprinkled with granola.

# Peach Frozen Yogurt

**SERVES 4**

*In this recipe, the gelatin acts as a stabilizer. As peaches can have a mild taste depending on their variety and ripeness, we suggest adding chopped dried apricots to give the flavor some additional punch.*

| | | |
|---|---|---|
| 1/2 cup | granulated sugar | 125 mL |
| 1/2 cup | milk | 125 mL |
| I tsp | unflavored gelatin | 5 mL |
| I tbsp | corn syrup | 15 mL |
| 1 1/2 lbs | peaches, peeled and sliced, about 6 small peaches | 750 g |
| 1/4 cup | finely chopped dried apricots | 50 mL |
| I cup | plain yogurt | 250 mL |
| 1/4 tsp | vanilla | I mL |

1. In a medium saucepan, stir together sugar, milk and gelatin. Let stand for 1 minute or until gelatin is softened.

2. Cook over low heat, stirring constantly, for 3 minutes or until gelatin is dissolved.

3. Transfer to a large bowl. Stir in corn syrup. Let cool to room temperature.

4. In a food processor or blender, purée peaches until smooth. Add apricots and pulse until smooth. Stir into milk mixture along with yogurt and vanilla. Cover and refrigerate until completely cold or overnight.

5. Stir peach mixture. Transfer to an ice cream maker and freeze according to manufacturer's instructions.

# Raspberry Buttermilk Ice Cream

**SERVES 2 TO 3**

*Despite its name, buttermilk is lower in fat than cream or even whole milk. But the incredible creamy taste of this frozen concoction will have you trying buttermilk with other partners, such as strawberries or peaches. Just substitute the same amount of your favorite fresh fruit for the amount of berries called for here. Strain the raspberries through a sieve just before freezing if you want to eliminate the seeds.*

| | | |
|---|---|---|
| I cup | fresh raspberries, or frozen, drained of syrup | 250 mL |
| I cup | buttermilk | 250 mL |
| ¾ cup | Simple Syrup (see recipe, page 23) | 175 mL |
| I | large ripe banana, sliced | I |

**1.** In a food processor or blender, purée raspberries, buttermilk, syrup and banana until smooth. Transfer to a bowl. Cover and refrigerate until completely cold or overnight.

**2.** Stir fruit mixture. Transfer to an ice cream maker and freeze according to manufacturer's instructions.

# Vanilla Frozen Yogurt

**SERVES 4 TO 6**

*Yogurt lovers will find this low-fat dessert delicious on its own — though it can also be dressed up for a party with a side of fresh berries or puréed apricots spiked with brandy.*

| | | |
|---|---|---|
| 1 1/2 cups | 1% milk | 375 mL |
| 1 tsp | unflavored gelatin | 5 mL |
| 1/2 cup | granulated sugar | 125 mL |
| 1 tsp | vanilla | 5 mL |
| 1 1/2 cups | plain low-fat yogurt | 375 mL |

1. In a small saucepan, combine milk with gelatin. Let stand for 1 minute or until gelatin is softened. Stir over low heat until gelatin is dissolved.

2. Stir in sugar and vanilla until sugar is dissolved. Transfer to a bowl. Let cool to room temperature. Cover and refrigerate until completely cold or overnight.

3. Stir in yogurt. Transfer to an ice cream maker and freeze according to manufacturer's instructions.

# Vanilla Ice Milk

**SERVES 3 OR 4**

*If you long for the taste of ice cream yet want to cut the fat, this ice milk gives you full value in the calcium and taste departments. Because of its lack of fat, ice milk tends to freeze rock-solid, so make sure you transfer it to the refrigerator for 15 minutes before serving. For added flavor, double the amount of pure vanilla extract. You can substitute low-fat chocolate milk for the skim milk for another taste treat.*

| 2 cups | skim milk | 500 mL |
| 1/2 cup | granulated sugar | 125 mL |
| 6 tbsp | powdered dried non-fat milk | 90 mL |
| 1 1/2 tsp | vanilla | 7 mL |

1. In a medium saucepan over low heat, stir together milk, sugar and powdered milk until the sugar and powdered milk are dissolved.

2. Stir in vanilla. Transfer to a bowl. Let cool to room temperature. Cover and refrigerate until completely cold or overnight.

3. Stir milk mixture. Transfer to an ice cream maker and freeze according to manufacturer's instructions.

# SAUCES

# Apple Brown Betty Sauce

**MAKES 3 CUPS (750 ML)**

*Granny Smith apples are our favorite for this recipe. We like it with Old-Fashioned Vanilla Ice Cream (see recipe, page 80) or Apple Brown Betty Ice Cream (see recipe, page 24).*

| | | |
|---|---|---|
| 2 tbsp | butter | 25 mL |
| 5 | apples, peeled, cored and sliced | 5 |
| 1/2 cup | packed brown sugar | 125 mL |
| 1 tbsp | ground cinnamon | 15 mL |
| 1/2 tsp | ground cloves | 2 mL |
| 1/2 tsp | ground nutmeg | 2 mL |

1. In a medium saucepan over low heat, melt butter. Add apples. Cook, stirring occasionally, for 4 minutes or until softened.

2. Stir in sugar, cinnamon, cloves and nutmeg. Cook, stirring often, for 5 minutes or until sugar is dissolved and apples are soft.

3. Serve hot or at room temperature over your favorite ice cream. Sauce will keep covered and refrigerated for up to 1 week.

# Banana Caramel Sauce

**SERVES 4 TO 6**

*These sautéed bananas are true comfort food — perfect as an accompaniment to Honey Vanilla Ice Cream (see recipe, page 64). They're also a yummy dessert on their own with only a little whipped cream on the side. You can substitute ground ginger for the crystallized ginger if you like.*

| | | |
|---|---|---|
| ¼ cup | unsalted butter | 50 mL |
| ¾ cup | packed brown sugar | 175 mL |
| I tsp | ground cinnamon | 5 mL |
| I tsp | crystallized ginger, finely chopped | 5 mL |
| ¼ tsp | ground nutmeg | I mL |
| 4 | firm but ripe bananas, peeled and sliced | 4 |

**I.** In a large saucepan over medium heat, melt butter. Stir in brown sugar and cook, stirring often, for 3 minutes or until bubbling.

**2.** Stir in cinnamon, ginger and nutmeg. Add bananas and cook, stirring, for 2 minutes or until heated through and tender. Spoon sauce over ice cream. Sauce will keep covered and refrigerated for up to 3 days.

# Blackberry Coulis

**MAKES 1 CUP (250 mL)**

*Our favorite thing about making coulis is that you can use almost any fruit to make a sophisticated sauce. Here, we've used blackberries and cassis to add that je ne sais quoi to our ice creams.*

| | | |
|---|---|---|
| 2 cups | fresh blackberries | 500 mL |
| ¼ cup | black currant (cassis) syrup | 50 mL |
| 2 tbsp | granulated sugar | 25 mL |

1. In a food processor or blender, purée blackberries, syrup and sugar until smooth.

2. Using the back of a wooden spoon, press through a fine sieve into a bowl to remove seeds.

3. Serve over your favorite ice cream. Sauce will keep covered and refrigerated for up to 1 week.

# Blueberry Sauce

**MAKES 2 CUPS
(500 ML)**

*Nothing is better than a hot fruit sauce poured over cold ice cream.
The heat from the sauce melts the ice cream to make a sweet and sinful
puddle on your plate.*

| | | |
|---|---|---|
| 3 cups | fresh blueberries | 750 mL |
| 1/4 cup | pure maple syrup | 50 mL |
| 1/2 tsp | ground cinnamon | 2 mL |

1. In a medium saucepan, combine blueberries with
   maple syrup. Bring to simmer. Cook over medium-low
   heat, stirring constantly, for 4 minutes. Remove from
   heat. Stir in cinnamon.

2. Serve hot or at room temperature over your favorite
   ice cream. Try peach ice cream or a decadent
   chocolate ice cream. Sauce will keep covered and
   refrigerated for up to 1 week.

# Cold Chocolate Espresso Sauce

**MAKES 1 1/2 CUPS (375 mL)**

*This sauce is a perfect topping for chocolate, vanilla or coffee ice cream. The best part is that it lasts longer than your store-bought latte.*

DOUBLE BOILER

| | | |
|---|---|---|
| 1 | package (8 oz/250 g) chocolate chips | 1 |
| 1 cup | whipping (35%) cream | 250 mL |
| 1 tbsp | cold brewed espresso | 15 mL |

1. In the top half of a double boiler over simmering water, stir together chocolate chips, cream and espresso until chocolate is melted.

2. Let cool to room temperature.

3. Serve hot over your favorite ice cream. Be as creative as you like with combinations. Sauce will keep covered and refrigerated for up to 3 days.

# Hot Butterscotch Sauce

*This sauce is the classic butterscotch sundae sauce. It is so delectable we guarantee you will enjoy it all immediately.*

**MAKES 2½ CUPS (625 mL)**

| | | |
|---|---|---|
| 1 cup | packed brown sugar | 250 mL |
| 1 cup | corn syrup | 250 mL |
| ¼ cup | unsalted butter | 50 mL |
| ¼ tsp | salt | 1 mL |
| ¾ cup | whipping (35%) cream | 175 mL |

1. In a medium saucepan, combine sugar, corn syrup, butter and salt. Cook over low heat, stirring constantly, until sugar is dissolved.

2. Increase heat to medium-high and bring to a boil.

3. Remove from heat. Carefully stir in cream, averting your face and holding the pan away from you and stirring until the mixture is smooth and foaming subsides. Be careful not to let it spatter.

4. Serve warm over your favorite ice cream. For a killer combo, serve hot over Dulce de Leche Ice Cream (see recipe, page 56) or chocolate ice cream. Sauce will keep covered and refrigerated for up to 1 week.

# Hot Fudge Sauce

**MAKES 3 CUPS
(750 mL)**

*Nothing says "classic combo" more than vanilla ice cream with hot fudge sauce. Whether you pour it over sundae fixings or just a single scoop, this lick-your-finger sauce will become an instant favorite.*

DOUBLE BOILER

| | | |
|---|---|---|
| 4 oz | bittersweet chocolate, chopped | 125 g |
| ½ cup | butter | 125 mL |
| ¾ cup | unsweetened cocoa powder | 175 mL |
| 1½ cups | granulated sugar | 375 mL |
| ½ cup | milk | 125 mL |
| ½ cup | whipping (35%) cream | 125 mL |

1. In the top half of a double boiler over simmering water, melt chocolate with butter, stirring constantly. Whisk in cocoa powder until smooth.

2. In a separate saucepan, mix together sugar, milk and cream. Cook over low heat, whisking constantly, until sugar is dissolved. Add chocolate mixture and cook, stirring often, until completely smooth and thick enough to coat the back of a wooden spoon.

3. Serve hot over chocolate, vanilla or any berry ice cream. Sauce will keep covered and refrigerated for up to 1 week.

# Mango Ginger Coulis

**MAKES 1 CUP
(250 mL)**

*Sometimes the best sauces are the simplest ones. Here, mangoes and ginger combine to make an elegant addition to fruity scoops of ice cream.*

| 2 cups | chopped peeled mango | 500 mL |
| ½ cup | crystallized ginger | 125 mL |
| | Juice of 1 lime | |

1. In a food processor or blender, purée mango, ginger and lime juice until smooth.

2. Chocolate Mousse Ice Cream (see recipe, page 45) goes well with this sauce, but you can serve it over your favorite ice cream or ice. Sauce will keep covered and refrigerated for up to 1 week.

# Pineapple Topping

*You'll start to salivate when you stir up this sauce on the stove. The buttery brown sugar is the perfect companion to the soft, slushy pineapple.*

**MAKES I CUP (250 mL)**

| | | |
|---|---|---|
| 2 tbsp | unsalted butter | 25 mL |
| 3 tbsp | packed brown sugar | 45 mL |
| I | can (10 oz/284 mL) crushed pineapple | I |
| 2 tbsp | dark rum or tequila | 25 mL |

1. In a medium saucepan over low heat, melt butter. Stir in brown sugar and pineapple. Bring to a simmer. Cook, stirring, until heated through.

2. Stir in rum. Cook, stirring occasionally, for 2 minutes more.

3. Serve warm over your favorite ice cream. It's especially delicious with vanilla. Sauce will keep covered and refrigerated for up to I week.

# Riesling Peach Coulis

**MAKES 1 CUP
(250 ML)**

*This sophisticated coulis is a great way to turn ordinary ice cream into something extraordinary. Try pooling this sauce underneath a scoop of ice cream and topping with a sprig of mint.*

| 2 cups | sliced peeled peaches | 500 mL |
| 1/2 cup | Riesling wine | 125 mL |
| 2 tbsp | granulated sugar | 25 mL |

1. In a food processor or blender, purée peaches, wine and sugar until smooth.

2. Serve over your favorite ice cream. Sauce will keep covered and refrigerated for up to 1 week.

# Sticky Sauce

*This is our version of the classic caramel sundae sauce. It's easy to whip up and elevates ice cream to a whole new level. It's so good, you'll be eating it straight from the pan.*

| | | |
|---|---|---|
| ½ cup | packed brown sugar | 125 mL |
| ⅓ cup | whipping (35%) cream | 75 mL |
| ¼ cup | butter | 50 mL |
| 1 tsp | vanilla | 5 mL |

1. In a medium saucepan, bring sugar, cream and butter to a boil, stirring, until smooth.

2. Reduce heat to low. Simmer for 5 minutes. Remove from heat. Stir in vanilla.

3. Serve hot or at room temperature as a topping for Classic Chocolate Ice Cream (see recipe, page 42) or drizzle over Baked Alaska (see recipe, page 81). Sauce will keep covered and refrigerated for up to 1 week.

# Strawberry Lime Coulis

*Although this sweet-and-sour coulis is the perfect topper to any single flavor ice cream, the zing of the lime is particularly refreshing when it hits a scoop of classic vanilla.*

| | | |
|---|---|---|
| 2 cups | sliced fresh strawberries | 500 mL |
| ¼ cup | granulated sugar | 50 mL |
| | Zest and juice of 1 lime | |

1. In a food processor or blender, purée strawberries, sugar and lime juice until smooth.

2. Using the back of a wooden spoon, press through a fine sieve into a bowl to remove seeds. Stir in lime zest. Sauce will keep covered and refrigerated for up to 1 week.

National Library of Canada Cataloguing in Publication

Linton, Marilyn
125 best ice cream recipes / Marilyn Linton and Tanya Linton.

Includes index.
ISBN 0-7788-0062-8

I. Ice cream, ices, etc.
I. Linton, Tanya  II. Title.  III. Title: One hundred twenty-five best ice cream recipes.

TX795.L55 2003      641.8'62      C2002-905887-2

# ❧ Index